The

BROKE-ASS BRIDE'S
WEDDING GUIDE

The

BROKE-ASS BRIDE'S
WEDDING GUIDE

Dana LaRue

Illustrations by Astrid Mueller

POTTER STYLE/PUBLISHERS

NEW YORK

The introduction and conclusion are created by Daffodil Campbell. "How to Feed 40
People for $3 Each" is reprinted here courtesy of Daffodil Campbell.

Library of Congress Cataloging-in-Publication Data
LaRue, Dana.
  Broke-ass bride's wedding guide / Dana LaRue.—First edition.
    pages cm
  Includes bibliographical references.
1. Weddings—Planning. I. Title.
  HQ745.L373 2013
  392.5—dc23   2013001708

ISBN 978-0-385-34510-1
eBook ISBN 978-0-385-34511-8

Printed in the U.S.A.

Book and cover design by Ashley Tucker
Book and cover illustrations by Astrid Mueller

10 9 8 7

First Edition

For **THE READERS**:
Without you, I'm nothing.

And for **MOM** and **DAD**,
with all my love.
I couldn't have asked for better,
and I'll never thank you enough.

For **PP**: 하늘 만큼 땅 만큼 사랑해

For **EMILY**, **CHRISTEN**, **MELLZAH**, and **LIZ**
(aka my bad-ass, broke-ass crew):
I wouldn't want to be in the trenches
with anyone else. Thank you for
having my back and making me look
good every day. But mostly, thank
you for your friendship.

For **HUNTER**, the OG Fresh Hubby

Love does not consist of gazing
at each other, but in looking outward
together in the same direction.

—**Antoine de Saint-Exupéry**

Introduction

Welcome, ye brave and eager souls. You are embarking on the wild and winding road toward marriage. It may not always be a pleasant journey. There may be storms. Dead ends. Forks in the road. Sleepless nights. There may even be a troll along the way in the form of a wayward future mother-in-law. But fear not, my intrepid friends.

I am here to guide you over the peaks and through the valleys of the wedding planning path. To teach you means of cunning and survival. To coax from you the inner bad-ass that will make your arrival at the end of the aisle as painless, rewarding, and (dare I say it) as much FUN as possible. Because, people, let's remember that, at the end of the day, *you're only planning a party.* Chances are, if you haven't lived under a rock for most of your life, you've done this before on a smaller scale. So breathe. You got this. I promise. And I'm here to help.

Here's the deal, though. I'm not going to bore you with all the regurgitated "budget wedding" advice you'll find in typical books and magazines. I'm not going to offer you second-rate replacements and compromises to help you pinch your pennies. I'm not going to expect you to be anything you're not. I won't let you wallow in feelings of deprivation or sacrifice as you plan your wedding. I mean it. I won't, so don't ask me to.

Here's what I *can* promise you. I will provide you with unique, outside-the-box tools and resources to stretch every dollar you spend to its fullest.

> Being a Broke-Ass Bride is not about how much you spend . . . it's how you spend it!

Because being a Broke-Ass Bride isn't about numbers and figures. It's not a price range or a pejorative term. It's certainly nothing to be ashamed of, or apologize for. *Embracing your inner Broke-Ass means using creativity as currency to rock a bad-ass wedding without breaking the bank.* This holds true regardless of your budget. It's about crafting a wedding that's an expression and extension of yourself, your style, and your values. Both of you, as a couple. A wedding that focuses as much on making the journey as enjoyable as the destination. The bottom line? Being a Broke-Ass Bride is not about *how much* you spend . . . it's *how* you spend it!

who the heck am i, anyway?

Oh, hi. I'm Dana. I was never the typical girl who'd dreamed of her wedding since childhood. I had cohabitated with my partner for several years. I didn't have many religious ties. Our families weren't pressuring us toward the aisle. But I wanted the wedding for three primary reasons:

1. To wear the pretty dress.
2. To throw the best party in history.
3. To sing my love for my partner, Hunter, to the universe in front of our nearest and dearest.

I'd been waiting for that ring for five long years, and I didn't want to have to compromise our vision for the wedding because of our financial limitations. So I made it my business to learn the art of wedding planning, in an effort to decode the mysteries and debunk the myths of the process and revise them until they fit me perfectly.

I devoured wedding websites, resources, and books with a voracious passion. But I quickly noticed a void in the market. Most of the budget books felt like generic "how to be cheap" guides. Their most creative advice was to "cut back on the guest list," which involved placing frugality above individuality, or felt more appropriate for a previous generation than for today's forward-thinking, progressive couples. Resources said "negotiate," but none told me *how*.

The one place I felt a sense of relief was in the blogosphere, where I was discovering sites full of unique inspiration and whisperings of more highly stylized, highly personalized events. My brain started churning with ideas of how I could revolutionize traditional wedding planning for myself. I was so inspired that I started my own blog. I figured that other people must be facing similar woes, and I wanted to help them the way others had helped me. With that, the Broke-Ass Bride was born, and through the site, I've shared my bad-ass, budget-friendly advice with countless brides around the globe. And I planned myself one HELL of a party in the process!

Sharing my experiences and innovative savings tricks online only magnified how much my husband and I grew both individually and as a team during the wedding process. After pulling off a wedding, I feel like I can plan and execute just about anything else. So why waste all that new knowledge on just one day, or on just *my* day?

In retrospect, wedding planning was much as I imagine business school to be; and when I walked down that aisle, I felt as if I should have been handed a diploma as well as a ring. Treat this here tome as your textbook *and* playbook. (I'd call it a workbook, but wedding planning should never feel like a chore.)

Read the parts of this book that speak to you, but if something doesn't, skip it! Not every piece of information or advice applies to every couple. Use the prompts I've included to help you find your path, log ideas and information, and springboard your own creativity. Learn from fellow Broke-Asses who not only survived their own wedding planning but also thrived as a result. Absorb all the tidbits and bytes of useful tools and tricks you'll find peppered throughout like the hungry spongeling that you are, my friend!

And listen, I am of the belief that love and marriage know no gender—so to my LGBTQ friends, welcome! The good news is that my wedding wisdom applies to you, regardless of gender or orientation. The bad news for any male readers is that, for the sake of consistency, I have written this book as though a ladyfriend is reading it. Please feel free to substitute the pronoun of your choice, with my hearty support!

the big picture

From research and negotiation to delegation and DIY, my wedding planning perspective is the alchemy of turning your obstacles into opportunities. You'll also be empowered with knowledge that you'll use long after you get hitched!

Your wedding isn't just one day. No carriage is gonna turn into a pumpkin at midnight, people. It is the beginning of your life as a married person. As a couple. As a team. The focus of your wedding should not be the expense. It is not about purchases, or timelines, or gratuity envelopes. It's not even about beautiful dresses and photographers and music. It is about you, your partner, your love and commitment. It's the beginning of a new phase of life, alongside a buddy who wants to be there with you every day. Which, you know . . . that's pretty awesome in and of itself.

Approaching the planning process with this in mind can help you save money, save the earth, and save your sanity. Whether you're learning to take baby steps outside of the box, or are ready to blow the lid off the whole thing, together we'll cut through the noise of typical wedding how-tos and sculpt a unique wedding event that reflects your personalities and gives your guests memorable insight into your relationship, all while keeping that price tag down to a number that's comfortable for you! We're making *frugal* the new "F" word—and kicking dowdy notions of thriftiness and savings-savvy to the curb while we craft an event that's truly *priceless*!

Screw tradition and let your unorthodox light shine, if old-school ceremony doesn't suit your style. Or revel in the ritual of convention and history, if that's what makes your heart sing. Don't confuse "expensive" with "better." And don't let self-consciousness impede your enjoyment of the process. There is no right or wrong, as long as you're straight-up with yourselves and don't compromise your truth.

DO honor your partner's wishes and include him in the decision making. DO just be your wonderful selves, and let the day be a reflection of that. DO surrender to the joy, breathe in the bliss, and let go. DO say please and thank you a lot. (It's simple, but so true.) Enjoy this rare moment, in which you really get to set yourself up for a fulfilling and fortunate future.

Now, doesn't that sound like a great way to view the planning process? Let's get this party started!

♡,
Dana

Breathe It All In

Oh, my God! *You're engaged!* That *really* happened. The magical moment you've been waiting for. The question came. The answer was yes. Your life status (and Facebook status) is changing, big time. You've gone from "committed" to "future Mrs." And that means a wedding is on the way. *Holy crap*, right?

No. Not holy crap. Not really. Not yet, at least.

Let's take a step back. Time to set some ground rules.

RULE #1: Bask in the afterglow!

Being engaged is just as important a phase as dating was, and as your marriage will be. Let yourselves settle into this one a bit before jumping forward. What that means exactly is for you to decide, but you have options:

- You can wait, and not tell anyone right away so that the two of you can just ride the rush of it together for a few sweet, privately happy days. Loll around in bed, order takeout, watch movies on the couch, make out heavily during said movies—you get the idea.
- You can simply share the good news with your nearest and dearest, and hold off on big public announcements for a little while, to ward off the rush of questions and expectations that almost always follow news of an impending marriage. *"Oh, my God, when?" "Where?" "I'm invited, right?" "Can I bring my new boyfriend?" "Who's in your bridal party?" "What should I wear?" "You're not going to do X, are you?" "You absolutely HAVE TO do Y and Z." "Here's a subscription to a bridal magazine that's sure to freak you out. ENJOY!"*

Regardless of when you let the masses know, keep in mind that *there is no rule that dictates how soon after the ring's on your finger you must begin formal planning or set a wedding date.* Do the engaged-and-loving-it thing for a while. Enjoy calling your partner your "fiancé(e)." It feels *prêt-tay fan-cé(e),* if you ask me. Trust me on this.

breaking the news

To be fair, ideally you should inform your parents, siblings, and closest friends first. That helps keep the likelihood of drama to a minimum, and a phone call or lunch date will suffice. After that, it's really as simple as changing your relationship status on Facebook to "engaged," sitting back, and watching the "likes" roll in. (But know that the same barrage of expectations and questions will proceed now, as well.) A newspaper announcement can make a fun keepsake, but for my money, it's more worthwhile to do it after the wedding—to announce the marriage officially.

the rules of engagement

Now is the time to sit down with your partner and discuss the *planning* of the wedding. *Note that I did not say discuss the wedding itself.* As tempting as that topic is, you'll have plenty of time for that later, trust me. In fact, you'll talk about it so much that at some point, and I promise you this, you'll want to gouge out your eyes, or the eyes of your beloved, or likely both. But right now, you and your intended need to hash out who wants to be responsible for what parts of the plan, and how involved either of you want to be with respect to the details.

"But, Dana!" you scream hysterically. "My partner isn't interested in any of the details!"

Well, I'm sorry, but that shizz is just plain unacceptable.

Okay, fine, that's not exactly true.

If you're a super–Type A personality, or you've been imagining your wedding in great detail from the moment you broke free from your mother's womb, then that may be exactly what you want—nay, *need*—from your partner. Hands-off, total agreement, nod-and-smile-style support.

If that doesn't describe you (we'll call you "Type Other"), you'll have to gently introduce your partner to the inevitability of his role in the researching, planning, organizing, spreadsheeting, financing, and handing-you-Kleenex-during-the-meltdowns-of-wedding-planning reality.

Okay, well. Maybe. Or, you could brainstorm his talents and interests and break up the duties accordingly, like a couple of people in love.

Who's better at organization? Who's a more skilled haggler? Who can research on the Internet like a boss? Who has a better eye for design?

Also, figure out who cares more about what. If you're a major audiophile, it follows that you'd be a better choice to plan the playlist and DJ or band. If your partner is a typography or graphics nerd, let him take the lead on the invitation selection or design. And for the elements that neither of you love, either scratch them from the plan, *because you're allowed to omit anything you wish—it's your wedding*—or suck it up, divide, and plan to mutually conquer. (P.S.: The aforementioned point about it being *your* wedding will be repeated ad nauseam—get used to it.)

And last, depending on your financial situation, this is a good time to discuss going on a "spending diet" to help you save for the wedding. And let's be real—if you're reading this book, you're probably a good candidate for that. Blogger Anna Newell Jones of "And Then We Saved" suggests that you and your partner write down your "needs" for each month (rent, utilities, insurance, groceries, gas, etc.), budget for those, and then give yourselves an allowance for extras such as entertainment, dining out, clothes, and the like. Anything left over each month goes into your savings for the wedding! The website Mint.com provides excellent budgeting and financial tracking software to help you identify where you're spending money each month and how to establish limits for yourself. It's a lifesaver!

Remember, you are a team. Thus, teamwork is to be expected. And there is no *i* in "teamwork," but there is an *ass* in "forced assistance." So brace yourselves for the fact that sometimes it will be super fun, and sometimes it will be a total drag, but thems the ropes of planning a wedding. If you're not in it to win it, maybe elope?

And if rewards-based systems work for you, work out one of those, too. Planning can be fun *and* mutually beneficial!

This is also a good time to discuss how to manage any possible disagreements that may come up. Find me a couple who agrees on every single aspect of their wedding from the get-go, and I'll show you a purple people eater.

As you begin the process, it's essential to understand that there are two people with two minds that are equally important, and that those minds will sometimes clash. This brings us to one of my favorite, and most commonly used, words in wedding planning: *compromise*. This means you'll have to get great at choosing your battles, and at being generous. And if it comes down to a stalemate between the two of you, find the least biased, most trustworthy third party possible to be your tie-breaker, or flip a coin and suck it up if you lose.

WHAT TO EXPECT WHEN YOU'RE ... ENGAGED

Questions: People want to know the what, when, where, and why immediately. Try to be as patient as possible, while providing the vaguest possible responses, until you've got serious plans in place, such as signed contracts, dates set in stone, and so on.

Overwhelming information: A quick search online will turn up thousands of sites, online mags, and blogs with tons of inspiration and eye candy. Each will have hard-and-fast rules of their own, and they'll all contain plenty of conflicting ideas and information. This is like

that moment in high school or college when you look around the new school, identify the cliques and clubs, and target the ones that align best with your values and style. Don't get pressured by loud claims of "trends" or "must-haves" or "colors of the year."

Coercion: The Wedding Industrial Complex, or WIC (see Glossary on page 244) is big and brawny, and its members are experts at manipulating young, curious, newbie bridal brains into believing that *want* supersedes *need* and that *spending* is one of your biggest keys to *success*. They make thriftiness sound cheap and dirty. They insinuate that *details* are *deadly serious*. They can infect your mind with "bloggability"—how bloggable will your wedding be? How do you ever expect to get it featured anywhere without the perfect mix of vendors, detail, and perfection?

It's MY wedding...
It's MY wedding...
It's MY wedding...

Wake-up call, people! Your wedding is for YOU, and its bloggability or whatnot should be the very least of your concerns—unless the only reason for you to throw a wedding is in the hope that Martha Stewart will validate your aesthetic sensibilities by allowing you to grace the pages of her magazine. In that case, Godspeed, good friend. I can probably be of little help to you.

RULE #2: Fan your fire for desire!

Put a moratorium on wedding talk one night per week. This is for your sanity and the sake of your relationship. Treat this night as gospel. Sacred space. Make planning a pariah. Do something—anything—fun together and just pretend you're not engaged at all. Or that you're already married. Whichever feels more natural. Keeping the romance alive is crucial during wedding planning, and couples often accidentally neglect it. Who wants to end up at the end of the aisle feeling totally romantically disconnected from his or her partner? The point is, ix-nay on the edding-way alk-tay, for realsies. And surprise your partner with something sweet once in a while, for no reason at all. You'll thank me later.

a pre-celebration celebration?

An engagement party is a great way to kick off a purposefully long engagement. It allows you to get your feet wet in the festive side of things, and can ease some of the "but I want attention / a party / to wear a pretty dress, and I want it now" anxiety that might otherwise jettison you into an early planning frenzy. There are as many ways to gather loved ones to celebrate your engagement as there are ways to plan a wedding, so the key is figuring out which party is right for you, if any at all.

And if, for whatever reason, you decide to get married within the next six months or earlier, you can skip the engagement party because, woman, you have a lot to do! Toast with Champagne, do a happy dance, and skip ahead to Chapter 2.

how to plan your perfect engagement party!

Engagement parties do bring up the question of etiquette. I'm all for wedding "rule" anarchy (even though I've included my own "rules" throughout this book—but, hey, it's my book, I make the rules . . . about rules, dammit!), but you might want to consider your guests and their easily bruised

---

SUGGESTED NON-WEDDING-RELATED-
Date-Night Ideas
FOR BROKE-ASSES

- Mini-golf
- Bowling
- Picnic in the park with delicious sandwiches, wine, and mandatory necking
- Clothing-optional board games or strip poker
- Movie night
- Anything you can find on one of those daily deals sites
- Stand-up comedy shows
- Happy hour
- Wine and cheese night at home
- Cook a meal together, try new recipes (like one from this book!), and dine by candlelight

. . . and remember, anything is more fun with a flask of booze stashed in your purse. And/or with fewer clothes. Get creative!

egos early on. Generally, if someone is invited to the engagement party, there's a level of expectation that he or she will be included as a wedding guest as well. If you're leaning toward a limited guest list for the actual nuptials, consider only your immediate family and closest friends for an intimate pre-party. And remember, a lot can change if you're planning a longer engagement. I don't want to harsh your mellow, but here are some real issues to consider:

FINANCIAL STABILITY: If you're counting on stowing away a little of each paycheck in your wedding fund, bear in mind that the economy is always in flux and employment situations can change at a moment's notice. I've seen many a hopefully huge wedding and its guest list get cut back by necessity because of job loss. It ain't pretty, but it's real life, kiddo. This could leave your engagement party attendees hanging without an invitation to the main event; and while one would hope that people are sympathetic to the fallout of economic instability, rational thought sometimes falls by the wayside in wedding-or-ego–related matters.

PLANNING FOR THE FUTURE: As tempting or fun as an engagement party may be, take a moment and really consider whether you'd rather spend your money on that, or save it for your wedding budget, honeymoon, or newlywedded life. If you can live without the betrothal bash and practice patience now, it may allow you to splurge on something more valuable to you later on.

the host with the most

Engagement parties usually come to life in one of two ways. If people close to you are offering to throw one for you, and you want to take them up on it, find out how much ownership they want over the theme and details. (Like everything else surrounding your wedding, *you don't have to accept help/input/ideas if it's not comfortable for you.*) Use your best judgment in terms of how much to share your preferences or ideas with them, and offer to assist as much as possible in order to show gratitude, keep an eye on things, and make sure they stay aligned with your values. This is a great chance to practice the art of saying "Thank you so much," and "That's a terrific idea, but actually, we'd prefer *this*." You'll need that skill, sister.

The other option is to throw your own party. If hosting in your home isn't an ideal location, look into local parks and picnic areas, recreation centers, or community halls. If you're having it in your hometown, see if the elementary, middle, or high school you attended would accommodate you, and give your guests a peek into your history as a bonus. When you can bring in your own food, party platters are the least effort-and-expense solution. Loads of restaurants offer large tray self-catering options, which they'll either deliver or you can pick up and handle the service yourself. Price out several options in your area and pick which best fits your taste and budget! Also check with any food trucks in your 'hood to see if they'll roll by your location and serve for an hour. See the "Hint" on page 30 for ways to control guest consumption when there's a menu in the mix!

For brides who are a bit more hands-on and don't mind getting their hands dirty, here are a few fun, budget-friendly DIY ideas:

kick-ass ideas for hosting your own broke-ass engagement fête!

A FIESTA-THEMED PICNIC IN THE PARK
- Mix up a big batch of margaritas and/or sangria (What's that, you say? You need a good recipe for that? See page 225—BOOM).
- Decorate with some *papel picado* (Mexican wedding flags) or colorful banners.
- Cut off the tops a few dollar-store sombreros, stick a Mason jar in the middle, and fill the jar with colorful farmer's market blooms.
- Put some Gipsy Kings on your iPod.
- Set up a build-your-own nacho/taco/burrito bar (see page 232). ¡Olé!

  HOT TIP: Make sure you're free to celebrate in a public park without a permit—and trust me, it's best to keep any adult beverages hidden away in plastic, colored cups.

A FAMILY-STYLE ITALIAN DINNER
- Cook up a heap of spaghetti (see page 228) or your favorite pasta dish (baked ziti bake-off, anyone?), and make a giant salad.
- Stick a bunch of candles in old wine bottles.
- Mix up a big batch of sangria (bulk drinks are your friend; I'm sure you're getting the hint).
- Put out some crusty bread in baskets with herbed butter in baby-food jars for centerpieces.
- Make up a playlist of Sinatra, Rosemary Clooney, and Tony Bennett. ¡Salud!

AN EXOTIC POTLUCK

- Pick a style of food, and ask each of your guests to bring a dish that suits. Explore the flavors of India, Greece, Mexico, Italy, Africa, or the Middle East!
- Provide drinks, some light appetizers, and a salad. Everybody wins.
- Have a multicultural dinner and assign each guest a different region of food to represent, for maximum variety.

A SUSHI-ROLLING SOIRÉE

- See the sushi setup on page 236 for a fun, interactive dining experience. Pick up inexpensive bamboo rolling mats, chopsticks, and seaweed sheets.
- Grab a few bottles of sake and some Japanese beer—and you've got yourself a party!

A WINE AND CHEESE TASTING PARTY

- Everyone brings a bottle of wine priced under $15 dollars.
- You supply a few hunks of cheese, cornichon pickles, olives, almonds, and crackers.
- Put each bottle of wine in a paper bag, number it, and hand out paper and pens for "tasting notes." Compare what flavors people identify and what they'd rate the wine price as, then do a big reveal!

those who can't do ... make reservations

Square away some tables or a private room at your favorite local restaurant and invite your favorite local people. There's absolutely nothing wrong with keeping it super-simple.

> *HINT: Speak with the management about negotiating a set, limited menu to keep your costs under control. For our rehearsal dinner, we worked out a deal with our local Mexican restaurant and planned a "burrito-only" menu to accompany prearranged orders of guacamole, quesadillas, chips, and salsa. We printed out easy menus for each place setting to let people know their options, and everyone loved it. No reason you can't do the same for your engagement party.*

And on that note, there's also no reason your guests can't pay for their own dinners at your engagement party. They're people who love you. They want to celebrate with you. If it means shelling out a few bones for that pleasure, they'll do it. Or they just won't come, and they'll miss all the fun.

In short, there's no reason not to celebrate, if you want to!

Take It from a Pro

Broke-Ass team member Liz Coopersmith of Silver Charm Events is our wedding planner–in–residence. Here's what she has to say about navigating the waters of newbie bridedom:

"You are not supposed to know how to do any of this, so you need to give yourself a break, right now. Odds are, this is the first time you've planned an event for 100+ people, and it will probably be one of the last. There is no inborn girl gene that is going to help you. There's just time and resources and learning, and making the best choices for you. The only pressure you have is the one that you're creating. You have everything that you need in order to get what you want. Remind yourself of that as many times as necessary.

It's funny, because the question my brides ask me the most is, 'Can I do this?' Whatever it is.

There's only one rule that I stand by in Wedding World: have the wedding that you want. Whatever that looks like to you. It doesn't matter if no one has done it before, it doesn't matter if everyone has done it before. It's your wedding, it's the only time you're going to have this expression of who the two of you are as a couple. Hold on to that.

So, when one of my brides asks me if she can do this or that, my answer is always yes. Of course. You just have to figure out how.

And I'm not saying there isn't a lot of outside pressure: 'Your wedding is the best day of your life.' 'Your wedding day is the first day of the rest of your life.' But today is the first day of the rest of your life, too. And so is tomorrow, and your wedding is not going to be the last 'best day' that you have."

Prioritize and Organize

First things first. Now that you've begun planning in earnest, I expect that you're balls deep in that *We're planning a wedding—now what?* feeling of hysteria. Fret not: nearly all couples come down with a nasty case of it, once the initial high of the proposal starts to wear off and the reality of planning a wedding starts to take hold. Repeat after me: it's going to be okay.

three steps in the right direction

STEP ONE: WE CAN HAVE LOTS OF FUN!

(Oh, what? Am I the only NKOTB here? I bet not!) Dispense with the typical checklists, and use wedding planning calendars sparingly. Instead, let's create a curriculum tailored for your priorities and with a time frame that suits your unique needs and desires as a couple.

When Hunter and I were first engaged, we were crazy overwhelmed. There were so many options, checklist items, possibilities that we didn't know where to start. So we sat down to hammer out what mattered most and what we could let go. We quickly realized that, to us, the wedding wasn't just "an event" or "one day"; rather, it was a new beginning and we wanted to kick it all off with that in mind.

Oh, and it had to be a bad-ass party! As we talked it over, our priorities revealed themselves: an authentic and personal outdoor ceremony; diverse cultural influences; an interactive experience for the guests; fly-ass music; free-flowing drinks; full and happy bellies; great photography; eco-mindfulness; and *fun*, fun times.

STEP TWO:
THERE'S SO MUCH WE CAN DO!

One of the most crucial pieces of advice I can offer any couple in the planning phase is for each of you to sit down and make your own lists ranking the typical wedding elements in order of personal priority. Is a fantastic DJ or a specific band the most important aspect for you? Or is splurging on the gown of your dreams in your top three? Compare notes. Together, try and narrow down your top three or four priorities, and give those items more weight in your budget. Similarly, compare which parts of the wedding experience matter the least to you, and come up with three or four things that you can scale back on seriously or omit altogether.

Think of it this way: your wedding budget is a bucket, and all the myriad wedding facets and ephemera are either rocks, pebbles, or sand. The best way to maximize what you can fit into your bucket is to put in the big rocks first (your highest priorities), then the pebbles

Saving on the When and Where

1 Remember that off-season or off-day events can save you bundles of money, so if exact timing falls into a gray area on your priorities list, pick a Friday in February or a Saturday brunch in November, and reap the rewards! Or get super-sneaky and book a Sunday over a federal holiday weekend. Boom—extra day-off bonus! Note that holiday travel may pose scheduling conflicts or increase travel costs for out-of-town guests, so weigh that possibility against the money it will save you before jumping to a decision.

2 Can you pay in cash, in one lump sum? Many people offer a cash discount or early payment benefit, but be sure you get a detailed contract with anyone you give money to upfront, whether it's a complete payment or a deposit. In fact, get a receipt *anytime* money changes hands.

3 All-inclusive wedding packages often contain buckets of savings, but they can also offer less flexibility or customization. Depending on your priorities and level of interest in decision making, this can be a pro or a con. You be the judge. Can you bundle items or services to create a discounted package that includes only what you want? Can't hurt to ask!

4 Having an outdoor wedding is naturally a beautiful choice, but there are often hidden costs, such as permits, generators, park rangers who need to be paid, tents, special lighting, heat lamps, even port-a-potties! Make sure to do your research and factor these into your budget before rushing into a decision about location. That being said, outdoor spaces can save you a bundle. Rental rates can be mercifully low in certain spots (or free if you're using a privately owned space), and the abundance of natural beauty can do more than hundreds of dollars of decor.

(the next highest priorities), and then fill in the gaps with whatever sand you have (your lowest priorities). Chances are, some sand won't fit in the bucket. But I promise, you won't miss it, as long as all the big rocks are in place.

Once you have your priorities in order, you can begin to figure out when it makes the most sense to have the wedding, and where. The longer the engagement, the more time you have for research, planning, and potential savings—but also the more time to second-guess, procrastinate, and go farther down the rabbit hole of wedding what-ifs. I alternated between bouts of total genius and bouts of utter madness in my twenty-month stint as a self-planning bride-to-be. And, yes, it took us seven months to settle on a venue. But in the end, I am grateful for having had the time. Hunter? Maybe not so much.

STEP THREE: IT'S JUST YOU AND ME!

Get familiar with the best wedding blogs in the business and subscribe to their RSS feeds. Why? (Besides the fact that I run one of said blogs and would love for you to get friendly?) Because we bloggers regularly run fabulous giveaways, from smaller elements like guest books or garters to huge-ticket items like custom dresses, photography packages, and even complete wedding packages!

One of the most rewarding aspects of running my site is the opportunities to gift couples with goodies they wouldn't necessarily splurge on for themselves—in part because when I was planning my own wedding, I was fortunate enough to be the lucky recipient of several contest winnings (including free photography from an award-winning company)! Don't give me that "But, I never win anything" business. You can't win if you don't play, so tell me, are ya feelin' lucky, kid?

Also, sign up for membership in some of the fabulous daily deal, designer, and sample sites that often feature wedding-specific sale events or other deals that will save you a bundle!

> HINT: Don't forget to check if they offer referral savings, so that anytime you share a deal and a friend buys it, you get credit toward a future purchase!

decoding destination weddings

Another thing to consider when venue hunting is whether you're going local or dreaming of a destination. Destination weddings can save you a bundle or cost a fortune. Generally, the less expensive packages, usually at beachy resorts or popular tourist destinations like Disney parks or Las Vegas, afford you less control over the look and feel of the wedding, and thereby offer little opportunity for customization, but these can be a great option for the more hands-off couples out there.

A benefit to vacation-style destinations is that you can transition straight to the honeymoon! And it may mean you can get married on a beach in the middle of winter, if you like.

If your destination is the hometown where you grew up, you might be able to obtain help from local family and friends to ease strain on your budget. Having the community pitch in can really amplify the personality and deepen the meaning of your wedding.

Bear in mind that the number of people willing and able to spend the money and time on travel to a destination event may be far fewer than those who would attend if you did it close to home. In some cases, you might see this as a good thing, and helpful for your budget!

A Handful of Great Savings Sites

DESIGNER-SPECIFIC SITES
Fab.com
Rue La La
Gilt
SeenOn
HauteLook
Editors' Closet
Ideeli
Beyond the Rack
Modnique
Ivory Trunk

DAILY-DEAL SITES
Groupon
LivingSocial
GiltCity
Yipit
Zozi
AmazonLocal
Travelzoo

BROKE-ASSES IN ACTION
Destination Weddings

"With my friends and family coming from either small towns in the West or all the way from the East Coast, and his family traveling from Australia, we knew that compromise and logistics were key. While we could have had one side of the pack travel all the way to Wyoming, where we lived, or to Perth—his family's base—we knew that something in between would be best. And cheapest for all involved. It was also a surefire way to keep the guest count to a minimum. So we picked Hawaii, which was almost directly in between our sides, and were able to keep the count down to 50 of our nearest and dearest. As a result, we got to throw a baller party, including our entire week at an amazeballz hotel, for just under $20,000. Sometimes thinking outside the box can be really beneficial. "
—**Broke-Ass Bride team member CHRISTEN MOYNIHAN**

Location can have a big impact on the price of your destination wedding. Resorts and hotels in, say, Mexico are going to run you a lot less for the whole megillah than hotels or resorts in Hawaii, for instance. And generally, all-inclusive resorts are a better deal than à la carte vacations. For an affordable stateside destination wedding, look to Vegas, friend! There are plenty of wedding packages for under $10K to be had!

Wanna get super-crafty? Look into renting a house in your preferred location with a yard that can double as your venue, and voilà! Sites like Airbnb, HomeAway, and VRBO are great resources for that. Your housing and your location are taken care of in one fell swoop! Even craftier? If you live in a popular vacation destination yourself, poke around and see if you can arrange a house swap with someone looking for a change of scene for the week, and trade spaces for the cost of travel alone. Just clear it with the owner beforehand—and look into insurance to keep both your behinds covered!

guest-listomania!

The guest list is always a hot-button topic, and one that is thus very hard to advise people on. I will say this: I'm sorry if your family is pressuring you about whom you do or don't invite. Family peace should always trump wedding details, but do try to keep things reasonable so that you feel connected to the people in attendance. *The guest list is not about appearances, it's about community.* The hard truth is, every person you invite will end up looking like a dollar sign to you at some point.

This is a good time to revisit your priorities. If having a big wedding is crucial to you, or you've got a huge family and hence a high number of guests you cannot live without, think about what areas of your wedding you can scale back on to make room. Serve heavy appetizers and dessert instead of a full meal. Make it a true community experience and throw a potluck wedding reception, inviting everyone to cook and bring his or her favorite dish in lieu of gifts. Keep your bar super-simple and affordable by serving big jugs of homemade punch (one virgin, one spiked). Or throw a bunch of blankets on the ground and have a laid-back picnic-style affair with boxed gourmet sandwiches, kettle chips, and cookies. There are plenty of ways to cut back on guest-count-related costs without sacrificing style or taste! More on this in Chapter 8.

In any case, you may find it helpful to create two or three potential guest lists:

1. Your "must" list: the people you absolutely cannot imagine not inviting—usually your very closest family and friends.

2. Your "want" list: the people you really, really hope to have at your wedding, but who are not quite as essential as your nearest and dearest.

3. Your "wish" list: the people you'd like to invite for one reason or another, but only if there's space.

Once you've determined your numbers and are ready to order (or make) your invitations, remember that, on average, roughly 10 to 20 percent of your invited guests will decline—which leaves you a little wiggle room to invite a few more guests than your ideal number. Depending on how many out-of-towners you have, and people's busy schedules, your acceptance rate can vary greatly. If you're getting married on or around a holiday or a very popular wedding date, you may have more declines because people have conflicts. (See the "Wedding Math Can Be Fun" box on page 42.)

If you plan in advance, you can always send out a second (or even third) wave of invitations once you've received enough RSVPs, and you've seen how your attendance list is shaking down.

HOT TIP: Number the backs of your invitations and create a spreadsheet matching name with number. Your silly aunt Sally will surely send her reply back to you, but somehow she can't be bothered to remember to put her name on it. Having that sneaky number reference system is a great way to foil the fools and keep your sanity. They even make invisible ink pens for this, in case you want to keep your method on the DL.

everything you need to know about STDs
(save-the-dates, people!)

Now I can hear your mother shrieking: "What about save-the-dates?" It's a tough call, but much like engagement party etiquette, it is best practice to send save-the-date notes (hilariously abbreviated as STDs in the wedding world) only to the people you're absolutely, 150 percent certain you'll be inviting to the wedding. If people start to nag you about it, and you're still not sure if you can accommodate them as guests, *wield the power of the white lie and politely say that you're still working out your numbers and will let them know the details as soon as you can.*

Your save-the-date notices should go out to guests somewhere between four months to a year prior to your wedding date. If you're getting married on a particularly popular wedding date or a holiday, get them out as early as possible. If you're getting married within four months, just forgo them or send an electronic postcard via one of the many free sites offering classy yet paperless invitation and notecard options, and focus on printed invites instead.

And don't sweat the STD style, people. You'll have proper invitations going out later that can be as formal or informal as you like. These days, it's perfectly acceptable to send out an e-card save-the-date or a simple post-card. If your mom starts hollering about how your grandma or reclusive uncle Dan doesn't know how to use the Internet, then send just a few postcards to the people who need hard copies and go paperless with the rest! You'll save money and earn some karma points with Mama Nature.

Whenever you send your STDs (or as soon as you set the details, if you're skipping that step), it's also a great time to set up your wedding website. You can direct people there on your save-the-date for updates and for further information. In fact, there are even a few companies that offer wedding websites alongside digital invitations, so you can take care of both in one fell swoop! Easy peasy lemon squeezy.

wedding math can be fun
CALCULATING YOUR INVITATION COUNT

If "**X**" = the number of people you actually want at your wedding,

THEN:

$X \times .2 = Y$ and $X + Y$ = the number of people you should invite.

NOW YOU TRY!

_____ × .2 = _____ and _____ + _____ = _____

TA-DA!

you've got a friendor...

Now that you've got your priorities straight and the nitty-gritty nailed down, check out what resources you have at your disposal. Do you have any especially crafty friends you can turn to for help, guidance, or hire? Using "friendors" can be a huge money saver, but make sure that...

- They'll be alright working at, rather than relaxing and enjoying, your wedding.
- You'll be alright with the same.
- You can count on them to stand and deliver.
- You have a backup plan.

Or you can be your own friendor! Do you or your partner have skills that can contribute to the wedding or be traded to offset costs? Look at your budget and priorities, and see where you can apply any of these cost-cutting cheats. More on this in Chapter 6.

To give you some idea of how friendors can help or harm your day, I'll share two examples from my own wedding. Our friends Gail and Robb owned a tea shop and specialized in tea-infused cocktails, and they offered to prepare and serve a pre-ceremony bevvie, which turned out to be a smash-hit among the guests. To this day, friends and family still comment on how a refreshing adult beverage really set the mood. Robb and Gail were prepared, arrived on time, and were professional and warm in their roles as temporary bartenders, and we couldn't have been more thankful that they were a part of our wedding day.

On the flip side, a friend (let's call him "Joe") offered to be the second shooter because our hired photographer was shooting solo. This would help ensure that no angles were missed, and someone would be covering both sides of the wedding party preparations ahead of time. Joe was a professional photographer, but he had no experience at weddings and wanted to give wedding photography a shot (pun intended—heyo!). We were grateful for his offer to help, and after we confirmed that he felt comfortable working the event, rather than partying as a guest, we did our best to prepare him with a detailed schedule for the day, contact numbers, and all addresses necessary. But when the day rolled around, Joe was unsure of where to be, was running late, and ran out of film halfway through the ceremony. We couldn't have anticipated those kinds of problems, and at the end of the day we were left with a friendor who performed only half of his job.

So weigh the pros and cons heavily before determining if the potential risks of using a friendor are worth the savings rewards. If you determine now which friends would make good friendors, you can approach them right away and possibly save yourself all the research time and effort that you would otherwise put into sourcing that vendor.

what's up, doc? the day-of coordinator

I rarely make absolute statements with regard to weddings, but I'm about to break that rule. *You cannot run your own wedding day.* The ability to just relax and enjoy is absolutely paramount, but even setting that aside, you're too close to it, sister! You can't stage-manage the show while you're starring in it. And you're already saving a ton of money by not hiring a full-scale wedding planner! So figure out a plan, early on.

Got a friend who lives for timelines and lists, and is annoyingly organized and prompt? Would she be willing to donate her time and energy to coordinating your day? Or is it worth the investment in a professional day-of coordinator (or DOC—wedding slang alert!) to gain the peace of mind from knowing that someone with more experience is in charge?

At the minimum, day-of assistance involves:

- Confirming that everyone is where he or she is supposed to be when it's time to be there (vendors and wedding party included).
- Handling last-minute requests and emergencies.
- Double-checking that the spaces are set up correctly and everything is in order.
- Delivering final payments and gratuities.
- Making sure everything is executed in a timely manner.

Quite frankly, it's the sort of work that would cripple me with ineptitude, and so I have a great deal of respect for those who can do it

Day-of Coordinators

I surveyed a selection of my readers who shopped for day-of coordinators in their area. Wanna know what they paid? And get a feel for the DOC experience? And find out whether it's all worth it? Hell, yeah, you do!

Q: WHY DID YOU CHOOSE A DAY-OF WEDDING PLANNER AS OPPOSED TO A TRADITIONAL WEDDING PLANNER?

"I wanted to work with my husband and my family (mostly my mother) to plan a wedding that truly felt like us, but I knew that I wanted to be able to enjoy the weekend of my wedding without dealing with any last-minute hassles or issues. My day-of planner gave us the chance to plan the wedding ourselves and make sure it felt authentic, but still gave me the freedom to hand everything over to her the weekend of the wedding to ensure that things ran smoothly." **—Alexandra**

"I'm cheap, and I'm a control freak. So, I considered a day-of planner because it would save us money, and because I wanted to handle all of the planning and projects on my own until the day of the wedding, when I'd be too busy to deal with it all." **—Dana Forman**

"I didn't need any help with the design aspect or crafting parts of the wedding—I had that all down. However, I did want someone to help run the show on the day. We had a small, family-only wedding (50 people), and I wanted everyone to be able to sit back and enjoy the ride! I wanted someone who would be able to enact my vision at our wedding, while the key players were getting dressed and having pictures taken. I didn't want my family to have to do all of that themselves." **—Sara Rich**

"Cost was a major factor, but I also had a very clear vision in my head of what I wanted things to look like on our wedding day—until I changed my mind, and had a new vision. I needed the flexibility of being able to guiltlessly change my mind and direction as my mind/circumstances/budget changed." —**Meredith Bono**

"Mostly I wanted to make sure that there would be someone people could call the day of with issues who was not me or my husband! I didn't want to have to worry about whether the vendors knew when to show up." —**Christine Nelson**

Q: WHAT WERE PRICES LIKE FOR DAY-OF COORDINATION SERVICES IN YOUR AREA?

"Prices in Sacramento were just around $1,000 for day-of coordination." —**Megan**

"I am from Providence, Rhode Island. I received quotes ranging from $700 to $1,500 from DOC services in both Providence and the metro Boston area." —**Mony Chea**

"We got a phenomenal deal at $600 for day-of services on the Eastern Shore in Maryland (1.5 hours outside D.C.). That said, she worked much more than just the day of (she reviewed contracts, met with our photographer at the venue for a walk-through a month before the wedding, etc.)." —**Alexandra**

"We lucked out and had a family friend who was looking to start a day-of planning business after catering weddings in metro Atlanta for ten years. We didn't have to price the service." —**Lara**

"I paid $600 in Columbus, Ohio. However, I was quoted $1,500–$2,000 by two different wedding planning companies in Columbus. I went with a small business with just one planner on staff. That price included two to three in-person meetings, unlimited e-mail and phone

consultations the entire time, and help connecting all of my vendors the month before the wedding. It also included the rehearsal the day before the wedding, and the DOC and her husband/assistant for the entire day of the wedding."
—Sara Rich

"I live in Chicago, and we're getting married in northern Michigan. I didn't see anything for less than $1,100 and up to $2,400. I ended up finding my DOC when she was having a sale, so she'll be just under $1,000, including her travel fees." **—Meredith Bono**

Q: DID YOU ULTIMATELY FEEL THAT THE SERVICES PROVIDED WERE WORTH THE PRICE?

"We paid our planner $400, and it was worth every dime! We both were able to spend the quality time with our family and friends, without worrying if people were being taken care of. And, it was absolutely essential through the reception! She kept our schedule for us, kept the DJ up to date with what was coming next, and just generally took care of everything." **—Lara**

"Absolutely worth the price. Our coordinator took the time to get to know us as a couple, kept us in the loop, provided us with references (and discounts) to excellent vendors, set up the table decor, and took care of last-minute issues. I was never so relaxed throughout the entirety of our wedding planning as I was on our wedding day. To me, that is worth a lot more than what we ended up paying." **—Megan**

"Most definitely. We had our wedding at our yacht club, so we had a lot of decorating to do. Our DOC facilitated all of that, and really kept the ball rolling all day. I also had a bad experience with our makeup artist finking out on our scheduled time. I forwarded the email to our DOC, and she contacted the MUA and got everything settled for me."
—Sara Rich

"Absolutely! For peace of mind it was worth every penny. My wedding day would not have been the same without the lovely ladies. I should mention I had TWO day-of coordinators and their intern on hand for my multi-ceremony wedding. They were hands on and always there to assist me with whatever I needed." —**Mony Chea**

"I think hiring a coordinator was one of the best decisions we made throughout the whole wedding process, and I would have happily paid three times the price (as it was, we tipped her very generously). Being able to relax and enjoy my wedding day, knowing that our coordinator was managing the decorations, dealing with our family, overseeing vendors, etc., was INVALUABLE. She was a pleasure to work with and helped my husband and me be totally present at our wedding without any need to worry about details. I cannot recommend a day-of planner (and mine in particular!) highly enough."
—**Alexandra**

with aplomb. At its greatest, a day-of coordinator is a professional who takes the reins a month or two prior to your wedding date and helps fill in the gaps, in addition to performing the aforementioned tasks and more. She's the fairy godmother of your big day, making everything appear to happen as if by magic—it's just that smooth. Some professional day-of planners offer firm packages, while others offer à la carte menus from which you can customize the level of support you desire.

The best way to source a day-of coordinator is to ask your budget-savvy friends with whom they've worked and let word of mouth be your guide. Or check local online message boards for referrals. And above all, meet with any candidates before committing so as to make sure you connect with your DOC and feel comfortable with that management style and energy. Your DOC is an extension of yourself on the big day, so you'll want to pick someone who represents you well.

budgeting: a cautionary tale

We're gonna get real here, so listen up, chickens.

Ahem. If I'm honest, we didn't actually have a budget—so to speak. (I know! I know! But hold off on the torches, I can explain!) We lacked a predictable income, so we had to wing it. We roughly said, "We feel on the outskirts of comfortable spending 'this much' money on the wedding, as a whole." Our families each chipped in early, which helped us establish a bottom line for how much we could realistically allocate, but it wasn't enough to cover the whole shebang (especially in Los Angeles), so we added a buffer fund of a few grand, for variable costs, and planned a very long engagement. Just to be safe. Rather than breaking down costs line by line in advance, we used the "big rocks" method I mentioned earlier: we tackled our biggest priorities first, negotiated them down to the lowest possible price, and looked at what we had left.

Each time a new purchase or deposit came around, we'd see where we stood and decide if it was worth it or not. It was risky business, I know that now. *And there are way more unexpected costs than anyone can imagine!* It's just the nature of the beast, but with extra-careful attention to detail it's possible to keep those to a minimum. And in the end, we did go beyond the buffered budget by a little bit—but not by much! The most important thing was, *we took on no new debt.*

I do not recommend this method, but our situation was one in which we weren't able to count on a certain amount of savings. We just had a vague figure and a boatload of hope, and a willingness to cut whatever corners we could. We carefully weighed where to splurge and where to save, and proceeded with caution. And it worked.

When all else fails, remember this: all it really takes to make a perfect wedding day is the price of a marriage license and the time to say "I do."

RULE #3: *As long as you end up married, you win.*

relying on the kindness of others

Whether you're relying on strangers (or family), handle the family and finances with grace:

- **Ditch what "the rules" dictate:** Ye olde traditions of the bride's side paying for "this" and the groom's side paying for "that" have become a bit antiquated in recent years, so those rules don't have to apply.
- **Have a frank conversation:** Make sure to speak openly with your families about your hopes and expectations for the wedding, and leave room in the conversation for them to offer assistance if it's within their means.
- **Manage your expectations:** In this day and age, a level of expectancy or entitlement regarding financial support can lead to a letdown, or worse, conflict and hurt feelings on both sides. If your families are on hard times (as so many have been in recent years), expecting them to cough up enough to cover your wedding isn't exactly practical or fair. So be respectful of the fact that everyone is struggling, and be super-grateful for any support they offer.

- **Brainstorm alternatives:** If they can't help financially, think of ways they can help in terms of investment of time or service. Can your mom sew? Would your dad be willing to research hotel room costs for your guests? Would your future father-in-law be able to trade carpentry work for a discounted service with one of your vendors? The gift of time and effort can be worth more than money, when time is tight.
- **Expect input for investment:** Take into consideration that sometimes when you accept financial support, those who contributed money may expect a certain amount of say in decisions about the guest list, design, or execution of your wedding. Some people I know have turned down money from their families because their desire for freedom in planning was greater than their desire for financial help. Others do just fine compromising with their family's wishes in exchange for the money. It's up to you.
- **The power of *please* and *thank you*:** Remember that there is no such thing as showing too much gratitude. Remind your family, friends, and hired help that you are thrilled to have their assistance as often as possible. And don't underestimate the power of the gesture—a simple bundle of flowers, a thoughtful batch of home-baked brownies, or a surprise bottle of wine are great, unexpected ways to say "I appreciate you," smooth over any bridezilla moments you may have (Oh, what, you don't think you will? Just wait), and generate loads of goodwill among your crew.

3

Who the hell are we? Let your wedding tell your story

So many design ideas, so little time

Dreaming up your theme

Double duty: killing two birds with one stone

A passion for fashion

Say less to the dress

Mining the interwebz for wedding inspiration

What you absolutely need at your wedding

Creating an atmosphere to get your guests in the mood

Divine Event Design

Look at yourself in the mirror. Smile, like you mean it. Oh, hi . . . you're pretty. Wouldn't it be nice to always look so nice?

Now ask yourself honestly: are you the type of gal who relishes the minutest of details? Were you secretly bookmarking wedding-related images on your computer for months or years before that ring showed up? Answer these questions based on who you really are, *not who you wish you could be* (trust me on this—been there, done that). Ask yourself truly: how much time and effort do you want these wedding plans to involve?

If you answered, "I'm in it to win it, D!" look back in that mirror and give yourself the crazy eye. Take a moment here and consider what you see, because this is an expression that your face will become all too familiar with during the ensuing months.

"Why?" you ask? Because the responsibility of self-designing a wedding will do that to you. The overflow of information, ideas, potential, craft projects, prices, details, and so on will make you crazy (sometimes). Your face will reflect said craziness at those times. This is simply a thing that's true. Don't try to fight it. The faster you let it wash over you, the faster it's gone. The longer you try to contain it, the bigger a hold it has on you.

But here's the thing. There is a dark and twisty rabbit hole full of details. Beware of feeling the "need to have." I probably slashed and burned hundreds of ideas about shiny objects, finishing touches, or charming twists on things because they were nonessential. These are the things you let go of when the wedding looms ever closer, and you're running out of time and money. But you know what's awesome? *You'll never even miss them.* I can't even remember half of my "need to haves" anymore. So, don't sweat the small stuff. Literally.

If you're less than design inclined, you might be able to avoid the crazy-eye phenomenon simply by being open. Flexibility with the details will allow for worlds of savings in terms of both sanity and cashola; but this all sort of harkens back to the Type A vs. Type Other discussion in Chapter 1.

Basically, it boils down to this: *The amount of control you crave is directly proportional to the amount of stress involved in planning.* You might think that retaining control will be more calming because there are fewer moving parts to worry about. Wrong! Unless you have super powers, but probably even not then.

Later in this chapter I tell you which items are truly essential for your fête, so you'll know you can safely step away from the full-size circus tent or the vintage Italian lace chair cover fantasies; but first, let's just dream freely and see what inspirations you can conjure up.

who the hell are we?
let your wedding tell your story

Now, even if you're as flexible about your wedding design as a master-level yogi, I still encourage you to examine ways you can infuse your wedding day with as much of you and your beloved's personal life story as possible, comfortable, and affordable. Let's examine why.

Your wedding guests likely comprise the following:

- People who know both of you well and have "loved you long time."

- People who know only one of you in that way and haven't gotten that insight into your partner (yet).

- People your families know and want present for various reasons but who don't particularly know either of you.

- People who used to know you well but haven't seen you in ages and don't know your partner either.
- People who are committed to going to upward of seven weddings this year. Already—and it's only March. They think nothing can surprise them, they've seen it all.

So let your wedding sing your song, and teach your guests something about the person you've become and the people you're becoming together, through the design of your day.

so many design ideas, so little time

Here's a lesson you must learn early, young grasshopper:

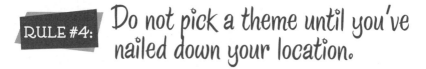

RULE #4: *Do not pick a theme until you've nailed down your location.*

We went through countless incarnations of our wedding design. For a long time I was sure we were having a natural, herbs-and-wine–themed wedding at a rustic vineyard in San Diego. Then we were positively doing a sunny fiesta-style affair at a destination in Mexico. After that it was an edgy, dark, *A Midsummer Night's Dream* theme at the Houdini House estate. But none of those locations worked out in the end, and none of the themes seemed right for any other locations we looked at. So when we finally found and booked the Bungalow Club, a "middle-terranean" restaurant (which has since been remodeled and renamed—sniffle) with colorful Moroccan tenting, lots of burgundy velvet, and hundreds of warm, glowing candles, the Magic Carpet Ride theme was born, and that one finally stuck.

I can't tell you how many hours of planning and clipping and research I did on those "weddings that never were." I was heartbroken to let some of those fantasy weddings go! So try to be patient and keep an open mind about the design. Usually, your venue will inform you of your theme when you get there. Just listen carefully, and it'll whisper its will into your heart.

A Wedding . . . Where?

We asked our readers to tell us about the most original and/or unique wedding venues they'd ever heard of.

"My husband's place of work hosts weddings—it's an airplane hangar." — **Rachel Covey Mostofizadeh**

"In Hawaii, you can get married on the side of a volcano." —**Brenda Araceli Munoz**

"I work part time at a funeral home, and they offered the use of their chapel." —**Emily Clark**

"We just got married in May at a historic carousel that overlooks a bay. The guests were able to ride while waiting for the bride! Also made for some amazing pictures . . ." —**Renée Matton**

"My husband and I met at Upright Citizens Brigade Theatre so we briefly considered getting married there, until we found out we could afford Disney." —**Mindy Marzec**

"The National Atomic Museum in Albuquerque, New Mexico. When looking for venues we thought it would be an amazing place to host our guests in the thick of history and innovation (especially since my now-husband's family are all engineers, and many have worked in the labs)." —**Amanda Vaughn**

"My sister just got invited to a wedding reception in a bowling alley!" —**Monica Z. Luarca**

"I am having my reception at the Butterfly Pavilion in Denver, Colorado. We get to do a butterfly release and our guests have full and private access to the place!" —**Emily Roth**

The lesson of Rule No. 4 applies to dresses, too. So the fifth rule is easy.

RULE #5: Do not, I repeat, do NOT buy a dress until you know where you're getting married.

There's nothing worse than a bride sweating through her taffeta on the beach, or freezing at her altar in the mountains. You can look, my dearies, but you can't touch. Not until that deposit puts your venue on lockdown.

dreaming up your theme

Figuring out your theme is as simple or as complicated as you want it to be. For some couples, it's enough to say "We're having an orange, chocolate, and sage green wedding" and that's the end of it. Anything they like, within the color scheme, is fair game. That's a very cost-effective method and a great way to keep things really simple. For others, it's "We're creating a hybrid *Twin Peaks*/LEGO theme but, like, at the circus!" That's a different story (though also kind of an awesome one). One of my very favorite real weddings we ever featured on the blog was inspired by the video game Minecraft. It was colorful and crafty and whimsical and fun, and perfectly *that couple.*

What did the Magic Carpet Ride theme mean to us? Basically, it was a bold sunset color palette accented by pops of fuchsia, peacock blue, and purple, with paper butterflies and candles everywhere. It honored our love of travel, adventure, and world cultures (especially Eastern art). It was a potpourri of ideas that made our hearts happy. We used carpet rides and Indian wedding processional imagery on our invitations, and we wrapped them in sari material. It was random. It was perfect—because it was a true reflection of our passions and taste.

How do you want to express yourself? What do you want to convey? Weddings are steadily trending toward a less uniform and matchy-

matchy feel and into a more creative and eclectic blend of aesthetics and colors. So let your style flag fly and enjoy setting an atmosphere that celebrates you!

Now that you've gotten your wheels turning in the theme-development department, here are some great cost-cutting measures to keep in mind as you start to flesh out the details. I go more in-depth on these soon enough, but let me introduce them early on:

- **Double-duty design:** Aim for a venue that can double as both your ceremony space and your reception area as a way to keep costs down. There are also plenty of ways to let one element serve as another, from escort cards doubling as favors to centerpieces doubling as dessert. We'll look at some specific examples of these on pages 61–62.
- **Re-up:** Try to plan on using your ceremony decor to spruce up your reception space. Could the florals on the ends of your church pews find new life as centerpieces on your dining tables, perhaps? What about bridal shower or engagement party decor making a repeat appearance to tie together all your bridal events?
- **Keep it simple:** The more generic the theme, the easier it is to control the cost. If you're content with sticking to a few basic colors, you'll save yourself from the vortex of customized details that a more particular theme can inspire.

Choosing a Theme

"I have always loved the colors of a peacock feather, and so it kind of just ended up being that without much discussion. We did, however, add a rustic element to it to balance it out and my fiancé gave his input on that. So rustic peacock it is!" —**Shauna Harris**

"We took important aspects from each of our heritages and combined them—he is French and English. I am mostly German and have several family members from New Orleans and that area. So our 'theme' or feel is French Quarter—green, purple, wrought iron, and fleurs-de-lis wherever we can get them in there . . . including charms on my bouquet and his boutonniere, and plant hangers with ivy spilling from them like the plants in boxes on the balconies in the French Quarter. One of our favors is Café du Monde coffee, and we're also making sea glass candy as a nod to the fact that we live at the beach." —**Rebekah Schell**

"We looked at blogs, vlogs, pictures, RSS feeds. We looked and looked and whatever we weren't sick of by the end of a month, we picked. Vintage bottles/doilies/burlap it is!" —**Emily Clark**

ME: I love theme parties. Let's have a themed reception.
JAMES: POWER RANGERS!
ME: What about Mad Tea Party?
JAMES: POWER RANGERS!
ME: In mine, there is the possibility of me considering a conversation about you wearing a top hat.
JAMES: Mad Tea Party it is!

—**Mallory Murphy Viscardi**

double duty: killing two birds with one stone

You can have strokes of savings genius by combining elements for more efficient design choices. Here are a couple great ideas on how to make decor magic while eliminating excess cost and effort! And because I'm such a nice lady, I've included instructions for most of these projects in Chapter 9 and in the Recipes (see page 224)!

CENTERPIECES

The accoutrement basket: Perfect for a wedding with rustic European flair! Place a basket at the center of each table, and fill with a bottle or two of wine, baguettes, baby-food jars stuffed with olives, pickles, and homemade herbed butter, sprigs of rosemary and sage, a bunch of grapes, maybe a hunk of cheese. Flank it with simple Mason jar candles, and your centerpiece is an adorable addition to the table that actually has purpose beyond appearance!

Dessert displays: Create a pedestal from any overturned cup with a plate on top (did someone say flea market fare?), and top it with cupcakes, pies, cookies, petits fours, or a miniature two-tier cake. At the end of the meal, invite your guests to dig in! Edibly incredible!

Plantable favors: Repot baby succulent cuttings and bunch six to eight of them together for an adorable, cohesive centerpiece. Each guest can take a little pot home at the end of the night as a favor!

TABLE NUMBERS

Bottle service: If you're serving wine at the tables during dinner, buy yourself a few cases of Two-Buck Chuck or hit up the 5-cent sale at BevMo!, and relabel the bottles with table names or numbers. Invite your guests to serve themselves once seated for dinner—couldn't be simpler!

Color-coding: Cut custom color napkins for each table from inexpensive cotton fabric, and designate the table destination by tone or pattern. It's a great way to add eclectic pops of color and ambience to an otherwise neutral room.

ESCORT CARDS

Snack attack: Tuck carrot and celery sticks into pint-size Mason jars with a splash of ranch dressing or a dollop of hummus at the bottom, and label each jar lid with a guest's name and table number. Guests can nibble on their veggies while they find their seats and wait for the festivities to resume. If temperature control is a concern and you don't want to risk limp veggies, substitute snack mix or candy instead.

Personalize it: Save on rentals and waste, and encourage guests to reuse their glassware, by providing personalized glassware they can easily keep track of. Thrift an eclectic mix of unique, vintage stemware and then use a paint-pen to write the names of your guests on each glass and their table numbers on the foot. They can take the glasses home with them as a favor, too, which makes this idea triply faboosh! Or do the same with ceramic dishware, using the instructions in Chapter 9.

a passion for fashion

As Rule No. 5 dictates, it is dangerous to put down dough on a dress when you haven't secured your location, theme, or date—mostly for obvious reasons. Once you know what season you're dealing with, what outdoor elements (if any) you might be contending with, and the mood, look, and feel of your wedding, your fashion sense will be able to more clearly home in on styles, textures, fabrics, and colors that work within those boundaries.

How and to what extent you inject your wedding wear with your personal style is up to you. But here are my five favorite quick ways to amp up your style profile!

1. CHOOSE COLOR OVER TRADITIONAL WHITE OR CREAM.
   My niece wore a gorgeous light gray gown for her black, white, and red winter wedding, and it was an eye-catching statement! Blush dresses are a stunning twist on traditional styles, too, but don't be afraid to go bold if that's what feels right!

FOUR TIPS FOR

Finding the Theme of Your Dreams!

1 *Remember Rule No. 4?* Do not pick a theme until you've nailed down your location. Consider outside-the-box venue possibilities, such as art galleries, rooftops, empty storefronts, parks, community centers, a friend's house/ yard, campgrounds, theaters—anywhere that speaks to your style can be a great location for a wedding. There are no rules. Or just let your city and/or state be the inspiration and design a wedding featuring what makes your location unique.

2 *What do you want the mood of your wedding to be?* Compile a list of words that describe how you want it to feel, and see if that clarifies things.

3 *Brainstorm your favorite colors.* Are there two or three that you and your partner agree on? Do they lend themselves to a mood or style or inspire ideas for one? Is there a symbol or shape that speaks to you? A pattern you love? Can you use that as a jumping-off point to create a theme?

4 *Are there passions that you and your partner share?* Anything from sports to video games to craft beer or wine, music(ians), countries, movies, travel, animals, gourmet food, TV shows? Basically any mutual hobby or interest can be worked into or become the center of your theme. Or combine two, one from each of you, and celebrate your individuality as well as your unity.

2. **PLAY WITH PRINTS**. I've seen jaw-droppingly beautiful print gowns with butterflies or tartan plaids, and gorgeous bridal parties donned all in seersucker. If you're not ready to give up the whole dress to a print, why not accent with a polka-dotted sash?

3. **GO WITH A THEME**. Beyond the endlessly popular *Mad Men* time warp, there is a whole world of style to explore, from Gatsby-esque Art Deco to flowy flower children. For beach weddings, why not put the men in linen pants and guayabera shirts, with the ladies in sundresses? Even serious steampunk-inspired fashion can look cooler than cool, and Elizabethan romance can go far beyond the costumey Renaissance Faire stigma you might imagine. Confession: I may have, at one point, tried to convince Hunter that we should dress as Mary Poppins and Bert from the carousel scene for our wedding. Dreamsicle!

4. **ACCESSORIES CAN ADD GREAT FLAIR**. These range from suspenders and spats to long gloves and pillbox hats, to top hats and tails, or fedoras and bow ties. I once saw a very dapper groom with a tiny fake bird on his shoulder. So charming!

5. **LET SALON STYLE SING YOUR SONG**. You can go full-on period with hair and makeup, or mix and match whatever generational styles make you feel most beautiful. Start clipping images from your favorite celebrity styles or magazine spreads and try on a few looks early on to find the right fit.

say less to the dress

No matter how you rock your own personal bridal style, wedding duds can rack up some serious cash. Lucky for you, I've rounded up some savvy ideas on cutting costs without sacrificing style!

1. **BUY OFF THE RACK**. Rather than squeezing yourself like a sausage into an often too-small sample size, and then having a bridal shop order a dress in your size, shop with sellers that are more likely to carry your size in store and be able to walk out with your gown in tow! Shops like J.Crew, BHLDN, The Limited, White House | Black Market, even Target, Macy's, JC Penney, and Nordstrom are great places to start looking. My bestie, Stacie, found her gorgeous Nicole Miller Grecian-style gown on a sale rack at JC Penney for $80. Fit her like a glove!

   For suits, if you like a clean modern look, stores like H&M, Zara, Express, and Banana Republic, and department stores like the ones listed above, are great resources for dapper duds in all styles and sizes. Vintage styles are best sourced in thrift shops, flea markets, and online vintage e-retailers but will likely need tailoring. If bespoke is your bag, you can also find e-tailors to custom-build period or modern suits for your groom, but it'll cost ya.

2. **SHOP ONLINE**. Bridal consigners, resellers, and indie designers abound online, and you can often score designer gowns for a fraction of the original price tag. Tradesy, PreOwnedWeddingDresses.com, Encore Bridal, and eBay are great websites to start your search. Message

boards on your favorite wedding websites will also often have sections where brides are selling off old gowns. And on sites featuring indie designers, like Etsy, you can usually find custom, quality dresses at completely affordable prices!

3. **SHOP WAREHOUSE OR CONVENTION CENTER BRIDAL SALES.** Filene's Basement is famous for its annual Running of the Brides—a run-on-the-bank-style-of-shopping event in which teams of women line up, sometimes days beforehand, to be the first to race in and find the best deals on piles of gowns, in all shapes and sizes, at discount prices. Charity events like Brides Against Breast Cancer tour the United States with hundreds to thousands of donated gowns—everything from high-end couture to more moderately priced brand names. And when you purchase from a charity sale, a portion of the proceeds goes to a good cause.

4. **SHOP WITH INDEPENDENT RETAILERS OR SEAMSTRESSES.** Indie retailers and businesses are a great resource for snagging unique, inexpensive styles, or for taking an ill-fitting resale or vintage gown and making it perfect for you—even building a dress from scratch! E-retailers like Dolly Couture, Unique Vintage, Hello Holiday, ModCloth, eShakti, and Shabby Apple are particularly useful for specialty dresses with personality that have off-the-rack or similar pricing. They're also great places to shop for bridesmaids' styles. For more custom work, Mignonette Bridal in Chicago will create bespoke gowns starting at around $1,400, for instance, which is an absolute steal.

5. **MAKE SOMETHING OLD YOUR SOMETHING NEW.** Whether your grandmother is trying to hand down her antique lace gown, or you stumble across the suit of your dreams, but a size too large, in a local vintage store, don't fret. A great seamstress or tailor can make thrifted clothes fit like a glove, or embellish a simple sheath with lace or beads from a family

heirloom. FitWel in Southern California does a bang-up job on menswear alterations, but you can lean on online reviews from sites like Yelp for help finding talented, affordable tailors and seamstresses wherever you might need them!

6. **HAVE AN EAGLE EYE FOR SALES.** Wherever you shop, they're bound to offer annual or semiannual sales, clearances, trunk shows, or special promotions. Sign up for e-mail lists, and follow your favorite shops on social media to keep abreast of the best deals possible.

7. **DIY SOME GLAM FACTOR.** Add some pizzazz to your ensemble by throwing in some unexpected pops of color and texture. You can use Mod Podge to coat your heels in glitter or decoupage them with paper prints you love. Add clip-on earrings to the front of your shoes for some baubly bling. Screen-printed details on ties, color-dyed crinoline under your skirt, or brooches attached to your bouquet ribbon are just the tip of the iceberg on ways you can doll up the details with DIY!

8. **WHY BUY WHEN YOU CAN RENT?** Sites like Rent the Runway and One Night Affair specialize in loaning out gently used dresses, from couture gowns to sassy LBDs, for a fraction of the purchase price. It's a great way to add a little eco-love to your big day and prevent closet-clutter from your gown for years to come. And for the gents, finding a tux rental is usually the most cost-effective way to go fully formal, if that's your bag.

Sites with Solutions

Pinterest
Lover.ly
My Wedding Concierge
LuxeFinds
Brides.com
TheKnot.com
Offbeat Bride
Weddingbee
Green Bride Guide
A Practical Wedding
Style Me Pretty
100layercake.com

Saving Face

Bridal makeup can cost a bundle, but no bride wants to sacrifice feeling her most beautiful on her big day, nor should she have to! Before you relegate yourself to drugstore makeup, consider some very savvy options:

• Which of your friends, coworkers, relatives, or heck, even local baristas do you find yourself often admiring for her facial handiwork? Test the waters by asking her to do a makeup session on you to "try out some looks you're considering," or invite her over for a private lesson in doing your own face. If things go well, make an offer and see if she'd be willing to be there for your big day!

• Hie thee to the mall, and indulge in one of the "free makeovers" at your favorite cosmetic counter. If you jibe with the sales associate, invite her to do your bridal makeup and inquire about her rate. If you don't hit it off or love the results, just swallow the cost of an inexpensive lip gloss and be on your merry way to another counter the next day/weekend. That's how I found my makeup gal—and I couldn't have been happier about how I looked! I highly recommend Laura Mercier for weddings—their foundations look natural in person and photograph really beautifully, plus their associates are well trained and very talented. I found my gal at Nordstrom, and she only charged a fraction of what a wedding makeup pro had quoted me!

• Or, make an appointment at a counter for the morning of your wedding. I know several girls who've done this at MAC with great results, and I did the same at Laura Mercier for my brother's wedding. Just don't forget to buy whatever lip color they use on you for touch-ups throughout the day, and tip generously!

A Love Letter to "Boobie Cutlets"

Dear adhesive stick-on silicone bra thingies,

Thank you for filling out my bustier on my wedding day and allowing me to go "bra-less" in my backless gown. Thank you for clinging to my tender bosom with such dedication throughout the evening, even when I was sweating my ass off on the dance floor. But thank you, most of all, for being the only thing between me and a serious nip-slip peep show in front of all my wedding guests and in many photos! I'll never forget you, good friends.

Love, Dana

Let this be a lesson, chicklets. If you're going strapless, and even if you have a strapless bra on under that gown, trust your good friend Dana and get yourself some stick-on boobs for safety's sake. My gown defied its fashion tape midway through the day, and yours might, too. Better to be safe than to suffer the agony of knowing Reverend Jim just got an eyeful of your breasticles, yes?

Speaking of undergarments, bring a few with you when gown shopping: strappy, strapless, push-up, or at least a sturdy convertible, so you can see what support works best in what gown. And let's never underestimate the power of a good pair of Spanx under . . . well, anything!

mining the interwebz for wedding inspiration

In "ye olden days," when bridal magazines were *the* source for inspiration, couples traditionally kept tearsheet binders where they'd file images and ideas. But with the surge in online wedding media, apps, blogs, and the like, having a digital inspiration board can be far more convenient and will allow for discoveries that are more unique (and affordable) than those typically found in bridal magazines.

Sites or apps like Pinterest, My Wedding Concierge, LuxeFinds, and Lover.ly are great resources for inspiration and allow for easy filing of ideas and images in ways that make sense to you. You can even create themed vision boards, like "Possible Bridesmaids Dresses" and share it with your bridal party so they can comment, vote on their favorites, or add their own ideas! Pinterest also allows you to take photos with your phone and upload them to your Pinboards, a trick that comes in handy during the inevitable moments when you see something in a store window and think *OMG, that would be amazing at my wedding*!

Yes, there comes a point at which every piece of data that passes by your eyes enters that part of your brain inextricably linked with the question: Can I somehow use *this* in my wedding? It's as if you're some sort of terminator-style android programmed to identify and assimilate all things pretty. Don't impulse-buy. Just file the idea and come back to it later, to decide if you really want it. You never know what else you'll discover in the meantime.

what you absolutely need at your wedding

While the WIC (see Glossary on page 244) would love for you to think there's a whole litany of things you *need* at your wedding, remember that they're writing for a consumer culture, and the truth is that you need only what you truly want. You can include or omit to your heart's desire, but here's a bare-bones outline of the *most common* things you'll find at weddings.

THE CEREMONY

- **SEATING**: Chairs, benches, pews, hay bales, colorful blankets on the ground. Or, if you're planning a very short and sweet ceremony, let them stand!

- **DECOR ALONG THE AISLE**: Flowers, a runner, candles, luminaries (paper bags with candles inside), or nothing at all.

- **DECOR AT THE ALTAR**: A table for whatever ritual supplies you may need, some flowers, a backdrop, empty frames hung with fishing line, or just let your venue speak for itself.

- **SOMETHING FOR THE BRIDAL PARTY TO CARRY DOWN THE AISLE**: Bouquets, wands, books, purses, floral pomanders, etc.

- **YOUR RINGS**: You know, for your fingers.

- **SOMETHING ON OR IN WHICH TO CARRY YOUR RINGS**: A pillow, a ceramic dish, a dog collar, a seashell with a ribbon hot glued into it, a Star Wars lunch box—whatever speaks to you!

THE RECEPTION

- **SEATING ARRANGEMENT INFORMATION**: Escort cards, a seating map, or something similar—only if you've chosen to assign seats or table numbers. Which also necessitates . . .

- **GUEST BOOK**: A literal book to sign, oathing stones (more on these in Chapter 4), a wishing tree, a framed engagement photo with an engravable signature mat for guests to sign, a leafless tree drawing on which guests leave their fingerprints to fill in the foliage along with their signatures, a Polaroid photo station with a blank book, markers, and tape. Be creative!

- **SOMETHING TO DENOTE TABLE NUMBERS**: Anything from the classic number in a stand to photo- or color-themed tables. We took pictures of our puppy on different stars on the Walk of Fame and assigned people to the corresponding celebrity via their escort cards.

- **TABLECLOTHS**: Not always essential, depending on the table. Inexpensive solutions include simple kraft paper coverings (which you can dress up with stamps—fun!), burlap, muslin, or other bulk fabric cut to size with pinking shears (see instructions on page 150).

- **CENTERPIECES**: Something in the center of the table to give it style. Can be floral/non-floral, edible or not, classy, elegant, funky or punky—it's totally up to you! Inspiration abounds on the Web.

- **DESSERT DISPLAY**: Most often a cake, but it can be anything! Cream puffs, donuts, milk and cookies? A Rice Krispie cake? Eat what you love.

- **GIFT TABLE**: Somewhere your guests can deposit their gifts for you. Include a box of some sort for them to drop cards into. Cards usually equal cash money. So you don't want to forget that.

Things you *may* need, depending on location:

IF OUTDOORS

- Extra lighting such as lanterns, string lights, antique lamps, etc.
- Arizona-style heater lamps, or shawls/blankets for your guests if it gets chilly.
- Fans, umbrellas, or parasols if it's extra warm or might rain.
- A tent, if the weather is really unpredictable.
- A generator, if your location is extremely remote and electricity is not provided.
- A park ranger (I know, I know). If you're using a public park, it may be required. Be sure to check into all their regulations before signing a contract; there can be many hidden fees.

EITHER INDOORS OR OUTDOORS

- Valet service, if parking is a problem at your location.
- Port-a-potties, if there are no public restrooms or a shortage of them available; they are available for rent—just don't forget to keep hand sanitizer, well, handy!

creating an atmosphere to get your guests in the mood

In a way, your guests are like babies: they'll relax and enjoy things most when they know what to expect. This goes not only for details that would affect their attire (weather, dress code, etc.) or travel but also for the style of party you're throwing. You would mentally prepare yourself differently for a buttoned-up, elegant affair than you would for a raging dance party, right? Right. So would your guests.

- **SET THE MOOD EARLY AND OFTEN:** Use your save-the-dates, invitations, and wedding website to reflect the tone as well as the design of your wedding. Fonts, images, and wording can all speak volumes about how casual or formal your event will be, so let creativity be your guide and have fun with it!

- **FOLLOW IT THROUGH ON THE BIG DAY:** Establish the tone right off the bat with smaller details. For instance, we played upbeat music and had a bar set up before the ceremony, with a refreshing and delicious signature cocktail, because we wanted to ease our guests into the "party mood" the minute they arrived. And as I said before, to this day, that bevvie remains one of the most oft-remarked-upon aspects of our day. Some couples offer inexpensive outdoor games to occupy the guests before the ceremony or during cocktail hour before dinnertime. If this sounds like your cup of tea, bust out the croquet mallets, boccie ball, lawn bowling set, or beanbag toss, and encourage some friendly competition!

- **PROVIDE "RELIEF" STATIONS:** Place convenience baskets in the bathrooms with items like Band-Aids, aspirin, antacids, hair clips, safety pins, static spray, tampons, mouthwash, dental floss, deodorant, clear nail polish (for nylon runs), and hand lotion—maybe even condoms, 'cause, ya know: romance *is* in the air. You can usually find most of these sundries affordably in the travel bin at your local pharmacy. (Not condoms, dude! Those are free at Planned Parenthood, though.) Save any hotel sewing kits or travel-size products and reuse them here, too.

- **PAMPER THEIR DANCING FEET:** Hoard dollar-store flip-flops in the summertime and put a basket of them near the dance floor with a note inviting your guests to "kick off their heels" and get down in casual comfort. Old Navy has amazing deals on flip-flops from time-to-time, too. Cute socks would do the trick, also.

- **SEND IN THE WELCOME WAGON:** If you're feeling really fancy, make a welcome bag for your out-of-town guests with an itinerary of the weekend's events, maps to each location, telephone numbers for taxi services, recommendations of places to eat and things to do in your area, and a personal thank-you to them for making the trip. Tourism or visitors centers often have pamphlets for local attractions and coupons for entry. Stock up on bottled water and individually packaged snacks at Costco or Sam's Club and toss a few in. We even made a CD mix of our favorite tunes about California for our out-of-town guests, and everybody loved them!

My goal here is (clearly) to give you tons of ideas, but don't feel pressured to do more than you're comfortable doing. At the end of the day, remember that despite what you see in print or blogs and hear from the WIC, there are really very few things you truly need for your wedding. At its most basic, it's you, your partner, a witness, an officiant, and a license. (That's $78 dollars in Los Angeles!) Everything else is just a bonus!

The Wedding Party

Your wedding party, should you choose to have one, is your royal entourage. Typically, your nearest and dearest friends and/or family are the ones chosen to stand alongside you while you make your solemn vows to the one you love. They also get to party like rock stars with you through the shower, bachelor/-ette parties, rehearsal dinner, morning of the wedding, moment of the wedding, and the whole night afterward.

Oh, what is one more distinct honor they're endowed with, as members of your chosen crew? Ridding themselves of a fat stack of Benjamins, all in the name of being a good friend, sibling, cousin, and so on. It ain't pretty, but it's true. Fear not, though, I'm here to save you from subjecting your bridal posse to unnecessary poverty at the hands of your wedding, and to help you keep fun times at a maximum.

who your crew, boo?

Like many things in this world, it's not the size of your wedding party that matters, but the motion of the . . . ocean? Wait, no. If this wedding party's a-rockin', don't come a- . . . Oh, hell, let's take this back a tick.

Ahem.

Like many things in this world, it's not the size of your wedding party that matters, but the quality of your crew. That's better. Now, the first question to ask yourselves is: How many people would you like in yours?

Gone are the days when the party has to match in size or gender on either side. While you may prefer a clean row of ladies and gents on either side, it is a growing, totally acceptable trend to have differing numbers and/or genders on both sides of the aisle. Enter the birth of the "bro's maid" and "groom's gal!" Is your first choice in a maid of honor a dude? Ordain him as your man of honor instead! Does your groom have a twin sister he can't imagine not being his best man? Welcome her as the best lady, and let her stand next to her bro! If there are only one or two people you really want by your side, but your partner has a few more besties in his inner circle, that's fine! Let's revisit the mantra: it's your wedding; you can do whatever suits you.

PUTTING EXPECTATIONS IN THEIR PLACE

The most important thing to remember is this: Asking people to join your wedding party is not a demand, it is a request—and if they decline, it doesn't mean they're rejecting you. There may be personal, or financial, or scheduling reasons precipitating their inability to participate.

Disappointment is a natural and acceptable reaction. Judgment and grudge-building are not. Keep your Bride- or Groomzilla locked tightly in its dungeon if this occurs.

I should know. It happened to us!

Hunter had asked his best friend from high school, Elliot, to be a groomsman, and Elliot was thrilled. But a few months before the wedding, Elliot got cast in a huge Broadway show (that would later go on to win a Tony), and the management would not allow him to take the time to fly to California for our wedding. Hunter was understanding, but still heartbroken. Then I had a brilliant idea! I secretly reached out to Elliot, and invited him to record and send me a video toast with which to surprise Hunter at the reception.

The result is captured in one of the most beautiful pictures from the night: Hunter crying and raising his pimp chalice (that's right, we had pimp chalices at our reception, yo!) to toast the video screen; there I was, grinning my ass off for pulling off having Elliot "be there" for Hunter.

popping "the question" creatively

My best girlfriend, Stacie, and I had overlapping engagements, which was an awesome, unplanned delight for us both—even though we were 2,000 miles apart throughout the process. Hers came first, and so did her wedding. I remember opening the mail one day and finding a card inviting me to be her maid of honor. A card that I could barely finish reading, thanks to the heart-bursting ugly cry that had taken over me in a moment of thrill, honor, and joy. It was so easy and simple, but it touched me deep in my heart of bestie hearts, and got the job done with thoughtful aplomb.

When it came time for me to select my bridal crew, I wanted to make it special in my own way. For my matron of honor (my sister

Consider When Curating Your Crew

Despite the fact that there is no right or wrong, there are some possible pitfalls to be on the watch for when you're selecting your wedding party. It can't be sunshine and unicorns all the time, friends.

1 *Politics:* Depending on your family or circle of closest friends, there's likely to be one or two who immediately assume they'll be ordained with the highest title. Or any title. And they may either cause a stink or be secretly hurt if they aren't awarded such. Can you trust them to put that aside and proudly wear the mantle of whatever title you give them? Perhaps you can find a special duty for your friend, such as usher or reader (or, as mentioned before, "shepherds of the rings" to assist with the ring-bowl passing from row to row through your audience). But if that's not possible, being there for your big day should be enough for them.

2 *Personality:* Consider whether anyone you're choosing to include might have an existing conflict with another member of the party, or if someone is likely to create drama where there is none, simply because that's a pattern of his or her personality. If personality conflicts exist, or may arise, do you trust these people to rise above the static to support you without involving you in their dramas? Can they put the past aside and bond together for this one special event? This is another risk vs. reward situation that you must weigh carefully to ensure that your wedding party is as nurturing, supportive, and low maintenance as possible. We've all seen the movie *Bridesmaids* by now, haven't we?

3 *Responsibility:* This is somewhat of an extension of number 2, but goes beyond petty arguments and status wars. Can you count on these people to be there for you? To show up on time? To maintain a presentable demeanor (i.e., not puking during the ceremony because they pre-partied with too much Champagne)? To represent you well in the face of everyone you know and love?

4 *Financial wellness:* As I mentioned before, standing up in a wedding can potentially add up to several thousands of dollars' worth of additional commitment, depending on the circumstance. Can you reasonably expect these people to come up with whatever scratch they'll need to be able to fulfill their duties, or are you willing to either cut corners to help them or contribute to their attendance? This one is super-important, as it's possible that some members of your party are involved in other weddings that year as well. We've all seen *27 Dresses*, haven't we?

5 *Yourself:* Do you thrive in a larger group, or do you feel most comfortable with just one or two super-close people? Or would you rather stand alone? What shape and size wedding party will make you most happy and at ease? Take care not to fall prey to the pressures of inviting more people than you want, or people you don't want, to be in your wedding party.

Dawn) and my best lady (bestie Stacie), I went to the dollar store and picked up blank, cutesy spiral-bound notebooks, which I used as storybooks to tell how we met and some of our most memorable moments. It ended with my asking them to hold their special positions at the altar by my side. I covered the pages in stickers and photos, and I used simple Magic Marker for the rest of the design. An artist I am not, but a story I know how to tell. (And I would hope, by now, you'd agree!) It made mementos that were fun to create and meant a lot to the ladies receiving them.

It was, however, a time-consuming labor of love at a time when, yes, *time* was at a premium for me. So for the other ladies, though no less special, I waited to ask in person. Thankfully, they all said yes.

I've heard tales of brides weaving as intricate a proposal for their maids as your partner might have made for you. It really is a matter of preference, taste, and what you can afford in terms of time or money. A simple phone call can do the trick, or a dinner out, a card in the

---

BROKE-ASSES IN ACTION

Popping "The Question"

We polled the Broke-Ass masses to see how they did it, and here's some of what they had to say!

. . . .

"I 'proposed' to my bridesmaids with a ring pop! It was great!"

—SHANNON EARWOOD DEFILIPPIS

"I ordered cute 'Will you be my MOH/ Bridesmaid' cards for each of my ladies. Then I made them a wooden gift box. I put a few little treats in them: mini-champagne bottle, lollipop, bag of Virginia peanuts (I'm a Virginia girl!), a monogrammed notebook, packet of tissues, and maybe something else. I hand-delivered each girl's box to her (including two out of state)."

—ASHLEY NICOLE REYNOLDS

"I put cards on bottles of Champagne that read 'For the day that I am to be a bride it would mean the world to me to have you sipping by my side; will you be my bridesmaid?'" —AMANDA POLLARD

"I custom-ordered 'Will You Be My Bridesmaid?' cards and personalized each one with a special pic of her and me, with a caption that said something along the lines of 'Let's make some more great memories together!' After each screamed and said yes, I gave them personalized keychains (that I ordered from a great Etsy shop) with their name and 'bridesmaid' engraved on them. Corny, but special." —JEN TRAUTMAN

mail, or a box of nostalgia from your history together will do. This really is not an area of your wedding that you need to allocate much stress, my sister. Breathe. They love you. They'll be thrilled you asked, no matter how you do it.

> HOT TIP: Once you've nailed down your crew and invited every-one, send around an introductory group e-mail providing every-one's contact information, a blurb about how you know them, a photo, and or a fun fact or two about each. This way they have a jumpstart on getting to know one another and, if relevant, can have group discussions about party plans, attire, and more!

the cost of friendship

Sure, it's a huge honor to be invited into anyone's wedding party, but there are a ton of sneaky costs involved that can quickly add great financial strain on your peeps, especially if your friend is one of those "universal bestie" types who gets invited into several wedding parties each year.

What goes into the price of wedding partydom, you ask? Well, let's examine the usual suspects.

- **ATTIRE**: Dress or suit/tux, shoes, socks or hose, undies, possibly even specialty bras or shapewear.

- **TRAVEL TO/FROM THE SHOWER AND/OR WEDDING**: This can be as simple as gas money and/or parking or as complicated as airfare and hotel for travelers from afar. In some circumstances, it can also mean forfeited income if your friends have to take time off from work. Yeowch.

- **SHOWER AND/OR WEDDING GIFTS**: Consider prohibiting your friends from buying one as a reprieve, what with all the other costs they're incurring. This is when the phrase "your presence is our present" comes in handy.

- **BACHELOR/-ETTE PARTY COSTS**: These may involve travel, gifts, transport, cover charges, dinner, drinks, entertainment, tips, and more.

- **SALON SERVICES**: This applies if you choose to line up a morning-of option for hairstyling, manicure/pedicure, or makeup—and if they choose to take you up on it but foot the bill themselves. Totally not essential, but also totally your prerogative.

- **TIME**: I've mentioned it above, but your wedding can take up a lot of your peeps' time. Especially if you'd like them to come dress-shopping with you, or you plan to enlist their help in day- or night-long crafting benders. Consider the value of their time as much as the value of their money when making plans that involve them, just to be *extra* nice.

Shaving off the excess

You can throw your entourage a proverbial bone, and help keep costs to a minimum, by following the "keep it simple" rule. That involves being as easygoing as possible; by putting your nearest and dearests' comfort level at a higher priority than what may have been your original vision; and above all, by being deeply grateful for their efforts and sacrifices to support you.

I'm here with some simple suggestions for lessening the financial strain on your peeps without sacrificing style or fun!

- Choose a color or scheme for their attire and let them select their dresses or suits within that palette. For the ladies, you can also specify a dress length, if you're keen on a more uniform hem. I've seen beautiful weddings with the party in all black, or various autumnal hues, but I've also seen adorably multicolor groups all in different pigments.

   One of my favorite weddings

bridezilla danger zone: THE CONTROL QUOTIENT

Hey, ladies and gents, it's one thing to tell your wedding party what to wear, down to the color of their shoes and socks. It's another thing to instruct the men on how exactly to fashion their facial hair or to ask your 'maids not to cut or dye their locks, grow out their bangs, and the like. You can laugh, my friends, but I've heard of these requests being made to people in wedding parties of yore. You're choosing your people because you love them for themselves. So while you can change their clothes, you cannot presume to change their style. Don't even think about it, Bridezilla!

had the bridesmaids all in white, each with a different, brightly colored pair of tights that matched their bouquets. The best part about letting them self-select their dresses is that it not only allows them to stay within a price range that's comfortable for them but it's also far more likely they'll pick a frock they'll wear again. Super win! (And I'll tell you what: I put a lot of time and effort into selecting "the perfect" dresses for my gals, but in retrospect, I would have been absolutely fine letting them choose their own. And I think they would have been happier, too.)

- Think outside the box when looking for dresses. Retailers like Nordstrom, Macy's, JC Penney, even Target (oh, excuse me. I should say Targé) have an amazing selection of dresses that are often more affordable and rewearable than your standard bridal-magazine fare. Plus, you and your bridesmaids can troll those stores for sales and score an even better deal than you dreamed!
- Give out-of-town friends a pass on being at every pre-wedding event. Skype them into your bridal shower, if necessary, and don't pressure them to fly in for your stag and hen parties. Repeat after me: it is not the end of the world if they miss it. Better they can pay their rent this month, yes?

alternative party and shower ideas for all budgets

It's a new day in the world of "last night out" parties. Gone are the times of gender-segregated nights of boozing, dancing, strip clubs, and karaoke. Couples are rewriting tradition and crafting bachelor/-ette events that speak to their taste and preference. Sometimes that means blending genders and exploring unique activities or escapes.

Here's a list of some of the less typical approaches to your stag or hen parties that might even save you some dough in the process!

- Troll daily deal sites for fun outings to turn into your bachelor/-ette fête. Many of those sites have added "experience" and "getaway" options whereby you can book fun and unusual adventures or escapes at a tremendous discount. Scavenger hunts, trapeze classes, paintball games, cooking classes, wine tastings, and pole-dancing classes are just a few of the literally hundreds of outings I've seen featured on these sites. Pair up a few to make a whole day of it! Or get out of town with one of the insane deals on weekend getaways.
- If a getaway is, indeed, more your speed, there are many options aside from the typical hotel suite or Las Vegas hootenanny. Sites like Airbnb can help you find unique short-term, affordable lodging options in people's guest homes, cabins, entire apartments or houses (or even a castle!).

- Learning experiences are a great bonding tool. Group classes—ranging from the physically oriented, such as burlesque dancing, trapeze, or skeet-shooting, to more creative courses, such as in sushi making or pottery throwing—are fun and unique alternatives to bar-hopping and strip clubs. Don't forget to try negotiating a group discount!
- How about a day at the races? A beach outing with a boat rental? A local amusement park? A laid-back day at the golf course? Dune buggy racing? Crashing the cheapest motel and divey-est dive bar in the smallest town within driving distance and taking over for the night? Camping in the woods, or on the beach, or in your backyard? Did someone say s'mores?

There's no limit to what you can do. All that matters is that it sounds fun and is affordable—for you and your crew! (You like my Dr. Seuss cadence there? Yeah, me, too. Ohhh, yeah, Miss Thing, I carried it through!)

It Never Hurts to Ask

(AND OTHER TIPS FOR THE HAPLESS HAGGLER)

I'm not gonna lie . . . negotiating used to intimidate me like nothing else. I'd stutter, stammer, lose my words, possibly giggle, definitely blush, and eventually melt into a puddle of self-deprecating ineptitude. I'd look at Hunter and sheepishly make "you talk" eyes. It took baby steps and several years of practice, but by starting small, I began to conquer the fear and, eventually, came to (gasp!) *enjoy* the art of negotiation. I'm now proud to call myself a negotiation ninja—wedding or otherwise!

I love reaping the rewards of negotiation. I haven't paid asking price for rent in years, thank you very much. And I can often be found haggling at the farmer's market near closing time to get my fruits and veggies. I recommend practicing nonbridal negotiation as much as possible before you go and meet with vendors—just to warm up your confidence and get your mojo rising. (Fact: role-playing at home is fun; start small with negotiating for kisses, and get sassier from there.)

staring into the eyes of the lion, and roaring!

In my research, I've noticed that most bridal resources encourage negotiation, but few offer solid suggestions on how best to approach the game. Yup, let's keep it real: *It is definitely a game.* I saved most of our money via hands-on negotiation, and I want you brides to feel empowered to fight the good fight for what you want. So I'm about to share some of my best tricks for handling the mighty task of haggling.

Many brides cringe at the thought of negotiating, but a bride who shows up "wearing the pants" as the role of negotiator (if you'll pardon the antiquated phrase) has one of three possible effects:

1. It commands respect.
2. It serves as a disarming distraction.
3. Or it doesn't faze the vendor at all.

None of those reactions puts you at risk, so why not give it a go?

Now, let's be straight. When you're "wearing the pants," I'm not talking about pushy, one-size-too-small-'cause-you-want-your-butt-to-look-right Bridezilla pants. That can trigger unspoken effect number 4: coming off like an asshat. I'm talking about wearing your most polished, respectful, savvy negotiator pants. Trust me ladies, they're much more flattering on you.

THE TOOLS OF THE TRADE

1. The key principle I operate under in many of life's situations is one my parents taught me, and reminded me of, all through my life: *It never hurts to ask.* The worst anyone could say is no, right? They could also surprise you with a *yes.* And wouldn't you rather be sure than miss an opportunity because of a lack of confidence? This is the hallmark of my approach to all negotiation.

2. If "it never hurts to ask" is the entrée to a negotiation, you must pair it with this side dish: *be nice*. It will make or break your deal. Vendors like to help nice people. They may not necessarily reciprocate your attitude. They might even act like you'll be *lucky* if they deign to accept your booking. But don't be distracted by their style. Always keep cool, positive, and strong. Soon you'll be killin' them with kindness (just like a good negotiation ninja should). But, I say, go beyond being nice.

3. Recognize them more as a potential friend than as a business deal. Get to know them, and relate to them on a human level. This business is about love, isn't it? The wedding industry is teeming with fantastic people worth knowing, and having them on your side will make them more inclined to have vested interest in your satisfaction. This isn't about manipulation; it's about being open. After all, wouldn't you rather have another friend at your wedding than just another vendor? A sense of camaraderie on your wedding day pays off in spades. To this day, I still get beers with friends who started out as my wedding vendors.

RULE #6: Research each vendor's role in your wedding and fully understand what goes into what they do.

Look into companies that suit your style, ascertain which you want to target, and evaluate which are most likely to be a good candidate for your event.

HINT: Google Docs time!

the value of research

Be careful not to let your desire for camaraderie overshadow your confidence in showing potential vendors that you know your stuff. There may be no guarantee they'll respect your knowledge, but at least they'll know better than to try pulling the wool over your eyes. Great expectations yield great results, so be confident and it will inspire them to have confidence in you.

Clearly, to show them that you know your stuff, you've got to *know your stuff*. The best way to get comfortable speaking on their level is to understand their product or service, inside and out.

PUT ON YOUR DETECTIVE HAT, SHERLOCK

It's time to get elementary with these vendors! Read through their sites and blogs closely, looking especially for information about how they approach their work, how they define their mission, what drew them to the profession, and so on. Read reviews on Yelp, WeddingWire, and other consumer-review sites. Message boards on wedding-related websites are a great source for referrals. Some pros even offer contact information for a few past clients, and you can ask specific questions.

Your goal is to get a great sense of their personality and style, which should be your first qualifiers in terms of finding a good fit. Once you've narrowed it down to a top three candidates for each service, query each for a price quote, indicating your preferred dates and needs, and be sure to let them know if you're flexible on those details in exchange for lower fees. Keep an eye on how long it takes each to respond, how thorough their response is, and how receptive they might seem to working within your budget.

KEY THINGS TO CONSIDER

Before you contact anyone, go in armed with the following questions answered.

1. **WHAT'S YOUR WEDDING DATE?** Will the vendor be in high demand during that season, or on that day of the week? Or are you planning an off-season and/or off-day wedding? Are you flexible on the date, or is your mind made up? The more flexible your date, the likelier you are to strike a deal. There's nothing wrong with a Friday night wedding, or a Sunday brunch affair. Some venues may even discount Sundays on a holiday weekend, which is essentially a Saturday, so don't be afraid to ask.

2. **HOW FLEXIBLE ARE THEY LIKELY TO BE?** Are they a promising new company, a talented small business, or an industry star? Do they need to build a portfolio, or can they afford to be picky? Many of the top, highly sought-after vendors are completely firm in their pricing, so know your audience before approaching, much less haggling, them.

3. **ARE YOU BEING REALISTIC?** If you can't afford their service, don't abuse the right to haggle. Young, fresh talent abounds in the industry—and you're likely to have greater success in striking a good deal with them. But there is one caveat: make sure their work is consistent and professional. Get a contract. There is more risk involved with less experienced talent, but that risk can easily translate into reward if you do your research ahead of time.

4. **WHAT REVIEWS CAN YOU FIND ONLINE ABOUT THEIR CUSTOMER SERVICE AND EMPLOYEES?** Do they offer past client testimonials? What's your experience with them—that is, response time, friendliness, professionalism? Sometimes you get what you pay for, and they need the business for a reason. Make sure you "click" with and trust whomever you book. It will make your life soooo much easier.

5. **WHAT SIMILAR COMPANIES ARE OUT THERE, AND WHAT ARE THEIR PRICING STRUCTURES?** Check the services included against one another to see how the best value shakes down. Ask potential vendors if they offer à la carte services or build-your-own packages. Get to know the competition, and try to seek out any specials or discounts. Blogs often have relationships with vendors who offer exclusive discounts to their readers (like mine!), so comb every corner of the Web that you can find. You never know what treasure you'll uncover!

6. **CAN YOU GET SPECIFIC?** Research everything possible about your desires and what they're worth, and then determine your bottom line. Know both your "dream price" and your absolute maximum, and be armed with specifics. Some of my easiest negotiations have been a result of a friendly reference to competitive company statistics. Let them know that they're your first choice, but go ahead and ask if they'll beat competitors' pricing or toss in an add-on.

"i'm gonna make him an offer he can't refuse"

If you can't find lower pricing to use as leverage and need a Hail Mary pass, make an offer. Even if a company advertises a specific price, they may respond to fair and respectfully made offers. *Respectfully,* people. This is more likely to be commonly accepted among smaller or newer companies with a need to build a portfolio or word of mouth. But the key is to be fair.

Be aware of the value of their time and goods. Try to get a sense of how many hours are involved in the job you're asking of them, and consider their overhead. Remember, everybody has to make a living. My favorite (and most successful) approach is: "[This] is what I need for my event, and [this] is my budget for this item/service. We'd love to work with your company because of [insert flattering but honest reason here, and make it specific], and I really hope we can work something out."

secret weapon time: barter

Like any good ninja, keep this one in your back pocket. It's your five-pointed star of negotiation. Offer a trade. That's right, the good old-fashioned *barter*. Whenever possible, offer something in exchange for the discount. Play to your (or your partner's) strengths. What can you do well for them?

Anything from cleaning their office or studio, or running errands and deliveries, to offering a trade of service like marketing, consulting, sewing, administration, publicity, or graphic or Web design might work, depending on the company and your offerings. Got a certified trade skill? Massage, yoga instruction, house painting, or dental work are just a few things that can be bartered. My sister used to massage away half her rent each month for her landlady, and got a whole wardrobe by working out the kinks in a local fashion designer's back.

Try and identify any needs your vendor may have, and politely offer some "free" assistance in exchange for a discount or full trade. When I fell in love with a dress outside my budget, I (half-jokingly) said, "I'm afraid it's just too much for me . . . but if you need any help around the office, I've got mad skills!" To my delight, an hour later, my phone rang and the designer offered me a fat discount in exchange for doing invoicing and cutting fabrics at her studio. I also traded marketing services, social media consulting, and more with other vendors for a savings of almost $20,000 on my wedding!

So when it comes to negotiations, start small—but be brave. After all, the worst they can say is no, right? If you approach with preparation, openness, and confidence on your side, you can be one bad-ass negotiator—and experience the empowerment of getting what you want at a price you can afford.

But, friends, if you're going to offer a trade of service, you better be able to back it up. Don't promise anything you can't deliver, either in talent or time. Taking on a barter can be as serious as having a second, part-time job—so be sure you're confident enough in your skills and your ability to meet (or hopefully exceed) their expectations. Nothing will sour a deal faster than you letting them down after they've gone out on a limb to make your dreams come true.

Newlywed Negotiation

Now that you're a full-fledged negotiation ninja, don't forget to apply this skill as often as possible in your newlywed life! From renting apartments to buying cars, you can (and should) bargain purchases and deals on a regular basis. Calling the plumber? Need your tire changed? Buying a house? Booking a getaway? Ask for a better price, know the market and competition, and barter your way to deal central! The same rules apply in life as they do to weddings, and you'll be surprised at how much you can save!

Haggling is like exercise: The more you do it, the easier it is. So keep your deal-making skills on point for use when appropriate!

A Less Than Phony Ceremony

When we wrote our ceremony, we were hell-bent on making it extremely personal and unique. *And because words don't cost a thing, we loved the freedom of having this be an aspect of the wedding that was not just free but also truly priceless.* The goal was to creatively and meaningfully set up and communicate the life we aimed to forge together. We figured, in making a solemn vow to each other, that it was best for our words and actions to embody our priorities and values as a couple. We invented symbolic gestures to replace ones that didn't resonate with us, and we borrowed inspiration from others and made the rituals our own. Our guests loved every minute. The best compliment we heard all night? "It was so YOU!"

Check with the rules of your state, as they vary greatly, but generally the only parameters for your ceremony are that you have a license to wed and you verbally agree to marry your partner. The rest is completely up to you. The ceremony can be religious or secular. It can be serious or funny. (It can, indeed, be both!) It can be partially or totally written by you or someone you know, modified from a book or a posting on the Web, or follow the traditional script. You can include cultural or spiritual rituals to your heart's desire, or omit them completely. Or make up a new ritual. But be sure to check your state's regulations on wedding ceremonies. A select few don't even require an officiant (in order to accommodate Quaker citizens, as their religion requires no official to be present), which gives you carte blanche to do whatever!

For us, writing the ceremony was a labor of love with diverse and personal touches, including vows to the universe (a pledge to care for the earth and its inhabitants) and vows to each other as we moved forward in life together.

on structure: the ceremony set list

Thankfully for you, creativity is your king—what you include or omit in your ceremony is up to you! No matter what you decide is right for your union, constructing your ceremony can be a bit overwhelming. Fear not, my friends! Here's a handy-dandy reference guide for the order of your ceremony, *based on our own ceremony,* to use or ignore as you see fit! I've included descriptions of some of the rituals referenced in the next section.

SAMPLE CEREMONY PROCEEDINGS

- Officiant takes position at top of aisle, signifies that guests should take their seats
- Processional begins, the bridal party enters
- Bridal processional begins
- Handing off of the bride; I personally did not love the idea of being "given away" at the altar as if I were an opinionless material possession, so we wrote in special wording as follows:

  OFFICIANT: Who presents this woman to be married today?
  MY FATHER: She gives herself freely, with her mother's and my enthusiastic support.

- Welcoming words and introduction
- Statement of intent (This is the "Do you . . . ?" "I do!" part. I recommend not skipping this. It's fun.)
- Group blessing (This is when the guests get their chance to say "We do!" in support of your union.)
- Explanation of the "Blessing of the Rings" and the beginning of their circulation. (This would also be a good time to do oathing stones or a memorial for family and friends not present.)
- Homily or reflections on marriage as a concept, union, or covenant
- Individual statements (our unique statements to each other)
- Shared vows (our traditionally structured, call-and-response vows)
- Additional ritual, if preferred (the loving cup, wine box ritual, unity candle ceremony)
- Reading (This also served as our vows to the universe. Our officiant explained our desire to make a statement of responsibility to the earth and its inhabitants by discussing the meaning of *Ubuntu*, a Swahili word meaning "My humanity is bound up in yours." He then read "Our Deepest Fear" by Marianne Williamson as we held hands and faced outward to the guests.)
- Bestowal of the rings

- Blessing and closing words
- Declaration of marriage
- Broom jumping, glass stomping, alternative celebratory ritual, if you like
- Recessional
- Receiving line (Or, if you'd rather, do this as a dinner-table circuit to get a little face time with each guest. I personally prefer the receiving line because it guarantees you won't miss anyone on his or her way out of the ceremony, and it allows you the freedom to enjoy your dinner and have a little time off your feet.)

a primer on wedding rituals from around the world

I'll begin with the basics. You may already be familiar with some of these. In fact, defining the first two is probably unnecessary, given their popularity—but hey, this *is* a reference book, after all. It's what you do, right?

UNITY CANDLE: Two candles are used to light a third. This can be done by you and your partner, or members of your respective families, to signify the unifying of your two families into a new one. Simple.

SAND CEREMONY: The same symbolism applies, but here, sand from two vessels is combined in a third. Often, couples choose sand of two different colors, but I think it's a fly twist to combine sand from the towns in which you grew up—if you, indeed, did grow up in a town with sand. The vessel is later placed somewhere in the home, to be gazed upon lovingly with fond remembrance. Or whatever.

SALT COVENANT: Another twist on the unity theme. Salt from two vessels is combined in a third. Why salt? It's all about adding flavor, preserving things, and melting ice—winning analogies for unity and marriage. Plus, you get the added bonus of using the salt to season your food as newlyweds. Fun fact: I'm a salt-aholic. I salt chocolate cake and cookies. Try it. You'll never go back.

Then there are the more worldly, historical traditions, commonly derived from specific cultures but easily adapted and applied to you, no matter from whence you or your people came:

HANDFASTING: A literal "tying of the knot," Celtic in origin. Your and your partner's hands are bound together with a rope throughout your vows, and then the rope is removed because you now hold the promises made to each other in your own hands. Awww, sweet.

THE LOVING CUP: Where my winos at? Hailing from the Celts, our friends in France, and the kiddush cup of the Jewish faith, each of you drinks from a common glass, sharing your first drink as a married couple. This signifies that you and your families are coming together (and perhaps eases a tiny bit of those at-the-altar nerves in the process). Feel free to replace wine with the beverage of your choice. My friends Lisa and Richard used tequila in a shot glass. Nice.

JUMPING THE BROOM: A tradition out of Africa, a broom is waved over the couple's heads to ward off evil spirits. They later hop over a broom before they exit down the aisle. In olden days, it signified a wife's commitment to cleaning the household she was then entering (cue guffaws, ladies), but nowadays it is symbolic of the creation of a new household together. It was also a common practice during the 1800s in the American South, when slaves were not legally allowed to marry. Instead, they performed this ritual in front of witnesses to signify their union. Nowadays, in some (not rad) states that don't yet legally recognize same-sex marriage, LGBTQ couples have adopted this (rad) practice for the same purpose, which I think is . . . rad.

BREAKING THE GLASS: Jewish in origin and done in remembrance of the destruction of the Holy Temple, either the groom or the couple together smashes a glass with his foot at the end of the ceremony. You may want to substitute a lightbulb, which is easier to break and makes a louder popping sound. Mazel Tov!

My personal favorites are rituals with the potential for guest interactions.

RULE #7: Treat your guests as part of a community rather than simply as an audience.

It makes the ceremony more engaging and memorable for everyone, and the fellowship it builds will spill over into your reception and your married life in the sweetest of ways.

OATHING STONE: The couple holds a stone while saying their vows, and it is believed that this act casts the vows into the stone as well—and thus into physical form. The stone can then be used at home as decor or a paperweight. Another option is to give each guest a small stone to hold throughout the ceremony, into which he or she wishes good blessings for you. The stones are collected postceremony and can be displayed in a vase at the reception, and later, your home.

> **BONUS:** Turn this into a guest book by asking your guests to autograph their stones with a Sharpie pen before depositing them in the vase. That's what I call killing two birds with . . . no, I'll spare you that pun. You're welcome.

BLESSING OF THE RINGS: Early in the ceremony, the rings are passed along from guest to guest, and everyone is invited to send a whispered wish or prayer for the couple with the rings as they make their way up to the altar. Ask a couple trusted friends to act as "shepherds of the rings," overseeing the passing of them from row to row and ensuring their safe return to the front in time for the big exchange. Best to tie the rings onto a pillow or into a dish to ensure they stay secure on their trip, though! One of my favorite photos from my ceremony is of my father whispering into our rings, tied into a seashell in his palm.

GROUP VOW TO THE COUPLE: In this ritual, the guests are invited to pledge their solemnity and support to the couple as a community of friends and family. When prompted to agree, your guests verbally commit to helping uphold your partnership before you make your vows to each other, by calling out "We do!"

WINE BOX RITUAL: A bottle of wine and a single glass are sealed in a box along with handwritten notes from each partner to the other. In the event that the marriage ever enters deep crisis, the box is to be opened, and the partners share the wine and read their letters to each other to remind them of the true nature of their love. We did this at our wedding, and invited each member of our bridal party to include a letter as well. I call it "In case of emergency." And if you never have cause to open it, all the better! On the flip side, of course, you have to be willing to open it if need be. Sometimes that's the hardest part.

Then there are the less ritualistic "honoring" moments in a ceremony, which pay homage to various people, causes, or beliefs.

IN MEMORIAM: The most common honor ritual, this is a moment in the ceremony in which any dear friends or family who've passed on are remembered and missed. This can be a moment of silence, an invocation of their spirits, or the placement of one flower on the altar for each person remembered.

SOCIAL STATEMENTS: Many couples have adopted a super-cool practice of including a marriage equality statement or gesture to show reverence for those who struggle to enjoy the same rights as couples who can legally marry. Robin Hitchcock, one of our real-bride contributors on the blog, and her husband incorporated this moment in their kiddush cup ritual by spilling a drop of wine, and using the following language in their ceremony:

In addition to sharing this wine as a blessing, Robin and Collin will also be spilling a drop of wine in recognition of those couples who cannot marry. This act honors the couples whose love is true, whose commitment is real, but who are not given the same rights as people as fortunate as Robin and Collin. This is not just a drop of wine, but a drop of hope, that someday soon those couples, too, will be able to experience this kind of awesomeness. Talk about "pouring one out for your homies"!

Bear in mind that these are just a taste of possible rituals you can weave into your ceremony. Use your imaginations and don't be scared to adapt these to better suit you or to come up with your own special sacrament. Whatever speaks to you, do!

your vows be stylin'!

Unless you're madly in love with the traditional wedding vows, feel free to play around with the tone and format, as there are several new styles picking up steam out there. But first, let's start with the basics:

TRADITIONAL VOW

I [name], take you [name], to be my [wife/husband/partner], to have and to hold from this day forward, for better or for worse, for richer, for poorer, in sickness and in health, to love and to cherish, from this day forward until death do us part.

VARIATIONS ON THAT THEME

Any variation on the above will work. Use that framework to give you structure, but freely omit or reword what doesn't work for you, or pepper in personal vows to each other. Don't be afraid to use humor in this, too! It's a chance to express your love and what you're willing to do to enact that love, in your unique way. It can be entertaining and meaningful at the same time. Light-hearted and serious. Blend the tones to your liking, and let your vows sing your true song.

I LOVE YOU BECAUSE...
BECAUSE I LOVE YOU

In this style of vow, each of you chooses (roughly) five statements to share, beginning with "I love you because . . ." and continuing with reasons you love your partner or character traits that you value greatly. After which, you begin (roughly) five more, beginning with "Because I love you . . ." and lead into the vows that you make to that person as a result of the love and commitment you have for your partner. You can choose to have the same reasons or promises as your partner, or each of you can tailor your own.

putting voice to your vows

Talk to your partner about whether you'd like to write your vows together or create distinct ones for each other that can be a surprise on the wedding day. If you choose to write separate vows, decide on a framework, such as an opening line and closing line. A friend of mine did this: They began by saying "I love you . . . " and ended by closing with "Thank you for choosing me." Hunter and I wrote a shared vow, but we also wanted to be able to write something special for each other. We added in a "personal statement" just before the vows, which solved the problem perfectly.

How you deliver your vows is up to you as well. Many couples hold hands, or incorporate the handfasting ritual for their vows. I stole an idea from a former bride's blog that I loved: Just before the vows, our officiant drew the infinity symbol (∞) on our right hands with his finger, and said the following:

> *Hunter and Dana, since it is your intention this day to join together in marriage, would you kindly extend your hands forward, palms open. In both of your palms, I make the sign of the infinity because love is about giving and receiving—a giving and receiving without end. My prayer for both of you is that from this day forward the giving and receiving of the love that you share will never end.* [To the crowd] *I invite you all to open up your hearts, and receive the gift they are about to give to each other. And know that as they give that gift, they are also giving to us all.*

We then placed our right hands over each other's hearts as we recited our vows to symbolize our protection of each other's heart. And because I'm so proud of our vows, I share them here with you! Feel free to steal or modify as you wish:

> *I, Dana, take you, Hunter, to be my lawfully wedded husband. To love you without reservation and to demonstrate that love in action, as well as word. To turn to you, and not* on *you, in times of trial; and to practice honest and thoughtful communication, especially when it's most difficult to do so. To challenge and inspire you to be all that I believe you can, and to welcome the same from you with an open heart. To make passion a priority, and faithfully work to entice and attract you through the years. I vow to trust in your love and put apology and forgiveness above ego. To take ownership of my health and to care for yours; to celebrate your joys and share your sorrows as long as we both shall live. From my hand to your heart, I thee wed.*

what not to vow

Be wary, friends, when crafting your vows, to ensure that you're not making any promises that you can't keep. While it's tempting and romantic to vow to your beloved that you will never hurt him, or always be by his side, it's not really something you can solemnly swear. So here's:

RULE #8: *Only make promises about that which is in your control.*

What is important is what you're willing to do to repair any pain or disappointments the messiness and unpredictability of human life will inevitably cause.

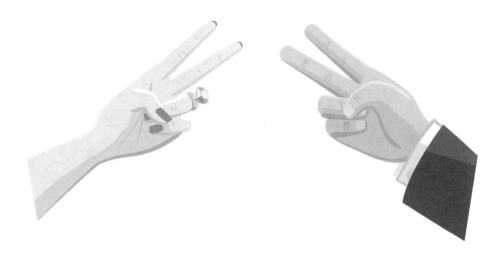

by the power vested in . . . whom?

One of the best things about our modern times is that almost anyone can become ordained to officiate your ceremony, giving you ultimate power to customize that experience to whatever level you desire. Ordination is free online through nondenominational sites like the Universal Life Church (ulc.net). Heck, your chosen officiant can even get ordained as a Lebowskian Dudeist minister and legally perform a marriage ceremony! (Google it.) In other words, it's up to you whether you'd like to have a religious official, someone from your circle of friends or family, your yoga instructor, a judge, or a perfect stranger preside over your ceremony. Just double-check with your state laws to make sure they allow for this.

Let's examine the ins and outs of who you choose, and why.

professional officiant *aka one with experience*	newbie *aka recently ordained online BFF*
• She likely owns a prefabricated or semi-customizable script, which can be a convenient and time-saving bonus if you're not looking for lots of bells and whistles.	• She knows you, probably loves you, and would be hugely honored to be involved.
• He is comfortable with public speaking.	• The ceremony can be fully customizable, and his relationship with you will infuse it with a special intimacy and the potential for fun anecdotal inserts.
• She will have enough emotional detachment to maintain a level of calm while performing your ceremony (i.e., not sob throughout because she "just loves you so much!").	• Since you're familiar with and trust her as a person, reliability, presentability, and the like are nothing to worry about.
• He is already ordained and knows how to handle the paperwork.	• He is likely to do it for free, as a gift to you and your partner.
• If she is of the same religious affiliation as yourselves, she will be familiar with the jargon and its customs.	

pros

what to look out for

professional officiant
aka one with experience

- Make sure you feel a personal, emotional, and/or spiritual connection when choosing an officiant. You want someone who puts you at ease so the ceremony is as intimate as possible (even if a "stranger" is performing it). Don't hesitate to interview a few folks to find the right match. Also (and not to be shallow), you want to make sure your officiant is presentable. It's like Internet dating—you can't always trust the photo online to represent how the person appears in real life. Fact: No one wants an officiant in sweatpants.

- How flexible is the officiant on his script? Check to be sure he is okay with omitting any verbiage you may be uncomfortable with, or including special flourishes that you prefer.

- Reliability: check her references to be sure the officiant has a history of being timely and appropriate. Or whatever level of inappropriate suits you. I know some of you out there aren't necessarily models of propriety, and that's cool with me, yo.

- Ask about his pricing, and secure a contract. Hiring an officiant adds another paid vendor to your list, so you'll want to treat that person as you would any other professional involved in your wedding.

newbie
aka recently ordained online BFF

- If she is very close to you emotionally, you might end up with an officiant who is crying too hard to make it through your vows.

- Unless you want to pen the ceremony yourselves, choose someone who is comfortable with the writing process. Work with that person to make sure any specifics you desire are included, and read the script with enough time for making revisions before the big day.

- Pick someone who will support your religious or spiritual views (or lack thereof) without hesitation or conflict.

- Be sure the person you choose is well acquainted with the process of signing and filing the paperwork after the wedding to make your marriage officially legal. (Seriously. Two separate couples I know were shocked to learn they weren't officially married because their paperwork wasn't filed appropriately after the wedding. See Broke-Asses in Action on page 107.)

- Choose someone comfortable enough with public speaking that she can deliver your ceremony with confidence and clarity. No one wants an officiant who is stuttering and red-faced out of fear.

7

The options: pros and cons

Alternative entertainment ideas

Let your tunes set the tone

Band vs. DJ vs.... Karaoke Machine?

"Don'tcha wanna dance? Say you wanna dance. Don'tcha wanna dance? DANCE." Hell, yes, you wanna dance! It's your wedding day, for rhythm's sake! I mean, if dancing is your thing, that is.

But whether you yourself like to boogie or not, you'll want some form of music at times for entertainment for your guests. There's the ceremony music, including your processional, bridal march, and recessional, plus any interstitial tunes you might want to incorporate during a ritual or as a special moment. Then there are the reception jams. At the very least, you'll want something playing in the background at the party to lend a festive mood.

Music is a highly personal, and often highly contentious, area of the wedding planning process. For those of you born with beats in your veins, the music selection and delivery process can become an extremely time-consuming and, sometimes, *all*-consuming item on your to-do list. This is often an area where couples encounter what I like to call "deal breakers syndrome"—a condition in which lines are drawn in the sand about particular decisions, and your ability to compromise is tested more willfully than in other areas of planning. Best of luck there, kids!

Let's take a look at the various ways to spice up your scene.

the options: pros and cons

The top three contenders for music are (generally): iTunes playlist, live music, and a professional DJ (or any mix of two or three of the above).

While the form in which your music is delivered can be a highly taste-driven choice for you and your partner, there are some specific financial and logistical benefits and drawbacks to consider before making any definite plans:

ITUNES PLAYLIST

PROS

- **Least expensive.** All you need is a decent music library, an iPod or laptop, an auxiliary cable, and you're good to go!

- **Minimal equipment.** Again, you don't need much. Note: Ask your venue if they have the speakers and sound equipment that will allow for this type of setup. If they don't, contact the biggest audiophiles in your social circle and inquire about borrowing their gear for the day of the wedding. Don't know any audiophiles? You can always rent.

- **Control.** You have the ultimate control as DJ of your own event, so each song selected is sure to represent your taste in tune-age to a T. No chances of an unwanted "Chicken Dance" creeping in here! You can even create multiple playlists for each part of your event: ceremony, cocktail hour, dinner, dancing, and so on to set the right mood for each. Precision music-ing!

CONS

- **Mood supervision.** You can't predict the mood of the room in advance, so there's a chance you'll run in to issues if the music feels unfit for certain moments. For instance, if you've programmed a slow dance ballad when the crowd is just starting to get wild, it might kill the mood on the dance floor at an inopportune time. And vice versa: if the crowd isn't warmed up enough yet, and a foot-stomping pulse-pounder is rocking the floor, people are unlikely to get up and dance. I've seen many a dance floor killed, and thusly a wedding end early, because of bad playlist flow. But that doesn't have to happen to you. Ask a few dance-loving friends in your circle to preview your mix and screen for any questionable choices or funky flow.

- **No accounting for taste.** If your tastes skew into unique niches that might not be universally appreciated, prepare to have that reflected in the mood as well. Your great aunt Edna might not be able to find her rhythm in the music of your favorite ska band, and don't you want her to be able to dance, too? I'm not saying you must eschew your favorite jams completely, just be sure to keep it diverse enough so there's something for everyone.

HOT TIP: Ask a friend (or a few, so they can rotate and have a chance to enjoy the party) whose tastes you trust to man your iTunes library and "guest DJ" rather than pre-setting a playlist. Or, for a less time-consuming favor request, you can even create playlists of suggested music, but allow the DJ to shuffle around as he or she sees fit, depending on the mood of your crowd. That way you're more likely to keep a healthy flow going rather than risk a start/stop that interferes with your atmosphere.

LIVE MUSIC

Live music is usually the most expensive option for weddings, but depending on your preference, it may be well worth the investment. Fear not, friends—with a little creative finagling, you can sneak some live tunes into your day without too much expense.

The best ways to keep costs down are to limit the size of the group, and limit the performance to just one portion of the festivities. A soloist, trio, or quartet are lovely choices for ceremony music, and you'd only have to pay for a couple hours of their time. Or if you prefer, bring out a full band to kick off the dance floor at the reception, but only use them for an hour or two and fill in the rest of the time with an iPod or DJ.

PROS

- **Play through the theme.** The right kind of band can really round out your theme and make it (quite literally) sing. A Dixieland-style band for your New Orleans theme, or a Sinatra-style crooner for your Vegas Rat Pack fête, can enhance the ambience that you've spent all this time trying to create. If you and your partner are fans of a particular band or era, let a cover band rock your party!

- **Promote a kickin' vibe.** Depending on the performers' style and presence, live music can inject your party with a different energy and create a richer mood than piped-in music can.

- **Fine-tune their set list.** You can select a musician or band that's entirely suited to your taste, and perhaps even request them to add specific songs to their repertoire that you find absolutely essential to your wedding experience.

- **Visual entertainment.** For nondancing types, there's something to watch—besides other people dancing.

CONS

- **Mo' musicians, mo' money.** Live musicians often cost more per hour, especially if there are several people in the band. Naturally, the more people in the band, the higher the cost.

- **Mo' mouths to feed.** You have to feed them. All of them. That's more money, too.

- **Mo' noise.** If your venue is small, a loud band might overpower it.

- **Union rules.** Performers have to take breaks from time to time, which can put lulls in your party when you don't really want them.

HOT TIP: Make sure you have a backup plan for tunes to fill the silence in your performers' set breaks. Some musicians will take care of this for you, but if not, an iPod is a cheap and easy solution.

BONUS TIP: Got a number of musical friends? Invite them all to participate in a round-robin of performances, and celebrate your talented friends while you dance the night away!

PROFESSIONAL DJ

PROS

- **Mood control.** A disc jockey can specialize in reading the room and can adjust the beats-per-minute with swift dexterity to keep the flow of the party going.

- **A musical mélange.** They come armed with a wide variety of music to suit all tastes.

- **Consistent rhythm.** Mixing one song into the next keeps energy up during song transitions.

- **Mix and mash.** If they're amazing, like mine (check out TheFlashdance.com, y'all), they might do mash-ups. What happens when your DJ mixes Kenny Rogers and Will Smith? *Everyone* gets up and dances, young and old!

CONS

- **Did you order a side of corn?** You need to screen your DJ carefully to avoid the cornball factor as much as possible. Some wedding DJs are just oozing with cheese. Are you looking for a DJ or a panini, people?

- **Cheap DJs sound cheap.** Their pricing can vary widely, so do your homework. This, along with photography, is a very "get what you pay for" service.

- **Mo' mouths to feed.** You have to feed him or her. But it's really only one extra person, so there's that.

alternative entertainment ideas

Spice up your night and delight your guests with unexpected acts (or activities) other than the average tunes and trots. Check out these ideas!

- Magician
- Stand-up comedy
- Karaoke

- Readings from literature, poetry, movies, etc.
  HINT: Turn this into a drinking game for a more interactive twist!
- Bingo
- Burlesque dancers
- Fire throwers
- Acrobats
- Swing dancers
- Cultural entertainment: Chinese dragon, luau dancers, folk dancers, etc.
- Tarot card readers
- Cigar-rolling station
- Caricature or silhouette artists
- Henna-tattoo station
- Dance motivators

let your tunes set the tone

Your ceremony music selections say a lot about you and your beloved; they present a splendid opportunity for you to craft a moment specific to your love story and life together. So do not feel pressured to "Here Comes the Bride" yourself down the aisle, if what you really crave is to glide toward the altar to "Walk on the Wild Side." I headed down the aisle to the ethereal intro to a favorite rock song of mine, "Mother's

BROKE-ASSES IN ACTION
Hot Tracks

Here are a few BAB-approved musical
suggestions from real-life readers!

PROCESSIONAL

"I Put a Spell on You," by Screamin' Jay Hawkins

"To Zion," by Trevor Hall

"Hoppípolla," by Sigur Rós, as performed by the Vitamin
String Quartet

"God Only Knows," by The Beach Boys

"Fidelity," by Regina Spektor

"Is This Love," by Bob Marley

"Your Song," by Elton John

"Somebody to Love," by Queen

BRIDAL MARCH

"I'm Under Your Spell," from *Buffy the Vampire Slayer* (on the
soundtrack to the episode "Once More, with Feeling")

"True Love Will Find You in the End," by Daniel Johnston

"Halo," by Beyoncé

"First Day of My Life," by Bright Eyes

"The Book of Love," by The Magnetic Fields

"Everlasting Light," by The Black Keys

"Mother's Eyes," by Jump, Little Children

RECESSIONAL

"I Melt with You," by Modern English

"Home," by Edward Sharpe and The Magnetic Zeros

"Signed, Sealed, Delivered," by Stevie Wonder

"This Will Be Our Year," by The Zombies

"Mr. Blue Sky," by Electric Light Orchestra

"You're My Best Friend," by Queen

FIRST DANCE

"Three Little Birds," by Bob Marley

"The Way I Am," by Ingrid Michaelson

"Parentheses," by The Blow

"Crazy Love," by Van Morrison

"A Kiss to Build a Dream On," by Louis Armstrong

"Maybe I'm Amazed," by Paul McCartney

"The Luckiest," by Ben Folds

"Wild Horses," by The Rolling Stones

"At Last," by Etta James

"I Will Follow You into the Dark," by Death Cab for Cutie

"What Is the Light?," by The Flaming Lips

FATHER-DAUGHTER/MOTHER-SON DANCE

"Gracie," by Ben Folds

"Daughter," by Loudon Wainwright III

"My Girl," by The Temptations

"Sweet Child O' Mine," by Guns N' Roses

"Be Still," by The Fray

"In My Life," by The Beatles

"The Way You Look Tonight," by Frank Sinatra

Eyes" by Jump, Little Children. It was the perfect length, I felt like I was walking in an underwater ballet, and I loved every second of it!

If it just wouldn't feel like a wedding without Pachelbel's *Canon,* then by all means, use it! You can always have a little more fun with the recessional song, if you like. So don't be afraid to pair something old with something new!

SIX MORE TIPS TO ROCK YOUR WEDDING LIKE A BOSS

1. **BE A SCREEN QUEEN:** Make sure to preview anyone you're considering hiring as thoroughly as possible, whether it's seeing a prospective band perform live at a local club or requesting a demo set from DJs on your shortlist. You want to be fully confident in their skills and presentation before committing to them—for better or worse.

2. **RULE THE ROOST:** Provide your band or DJ with a "must-play" list—and include the digital files of any essential songs such as the first dance or cake cutting jams so they're more than prepared. On the flip side, if the idea of the Macarena at your wedding makes you want to die of embarrassment or you can't stand a certain popular musician, don't be afraid to create a "do not play" list.

3. **KNOW THE LIMITS:** Be sure to double check any contract before you sign to make sure it covers the correct timing of your event, the number of hours you're booking the vendors for as well as their mandated breaks, and any overtime agreements should your party run long.

4. **HELLO? HELLO? ECHO! ECHO!:** Check the acoustics of your venue before finalizing any plans for music. The size of the space and surface structure can strongly affect what kind of sound system you'll need or how rockin' of a band you hire.

5. **HOUSE RULES**: Check with your venue on any limits to where and when amplified music can be played. Many spaces in residential areas or public parks either won't allow for it at all or have strict cut-off times. Last thing you want is a neighbor callin' the cops because your party is bumpin' too loudly!

6. **CONNECT WITH YOUR PARTNER**: During your first dance, fend off any "we're being watched" nerves and enhance the romance by focusing on each other as much as possible. Kiss, swoon, and giggle. Say "I love you." A lot. Likewise, during your parent-child dance, connect with your mother or father and thank them for everything they did to get you to that moment, letting them know how grateful you are to have them there. It's a few minutes that can be worth a lifetime of happy memories. So enjoy it.

8

Feeding the Locals

Food and beverage costs most often account for around 50 percent of your total budget. For good reason, too! Weddings at which the guests go hungry or thirsty are no fun for anyone. This isn't to say that a multicourse gourmet meal is necessary or expected, but hungry people get cranky. Cranky people leave parties early. Don't turn your guests into party poopers, dudes. It's not worth the money you'll save.

RULE #9: Never let your guests go hungry!

If you're on a serious shoestring, it's perfectly acceptable to scale back on your cuisine offerings and do a simple "dessert only" or "cake and Champagne" reception. Just be sure to include that information on the invitation, so your guests know to eat beforehand. It's all about managing expectations.

I once went to a wedding where only cheese trays and nuts were served. It was an absolutely lovely wedding, and everyone was having a fantastic time. But after a couple of hours with the open bar and dancing, the natives were getting restless, so one of the guests took charge and called Pizza Hut to have twenty pies delivered, on him. The party was injected with fresh energy and went on for hours to come.

Lucky for you, you've got this book to teach you some easy ways to inexpensively feed large groups of people so you and your guests will be good to go into the wee hours!

what to eat?

It's totally up to you! But I recommend serving food you like. That always helps. If you're having your reception at a venue that requires you to use their kitchen or catering service, as is often the case in restaurants and hotels or banquet halls, your options are limited. But if you have the freedom to choose, here are my suggestions [drumroll, please]:

SIX THINGS TO CONSIDER WHEN PLANNING YOUR RECEPTION FOOD

1. **WHAT TIME OF DAY IS YOUR RECEPTION?** You can get away with serving lighter fare for brunch or lunch than for dinner. Although, I personally think the idea of serving breakfast for

dinner is a fantastic and unexpected twist on an evening wedding meal. And eggs be cheap, yo. Did someone say maple syrup fountain? Yep. I just went there.

2. **DOES YOUR THEME LEND ITSELF TO A SPECIFIC TYPE OF CUISINE?** It can be really fun to design your menu to complement your decor. For your Asian-inspired Double Happiness theme, serve orange chicken and fried rice. A big batch of spaghetti or lasagna and salad rounds out the Tuscan Rustic reception style. Having a Hawaiian-Style Luau? Why not go whole hog and roast a pig? Keeping the style of food consistent can add up to savings because of crossover ingredients and seasonings.

3. **HOW LENIENT ARE YOU ON SERVING STYLE?** Being flexible can make a very big impact on your budget. If you want a full meal, served plated, in courses, you'll have to account for the extra serving staff, bussers, plates, and so on, which add up to more dollars. It's nice to serve this way because everyone can remain seated throughout the meal, and it eliminates the sometimes awkward buffet-line problems, but you're paying for this luxury, friend. Buffets save a lot of dough (food puns abound!) because you need far less staff, but depending on the caterer, sometimes the quality of the food can suffer as a result. Buffets do allow you to offer more variety, however. If you go this route, why not offer stations with different ethnic cuisines? Or employ an interactive element, such as a designer mashed-potato bar with various toppings the guests can help themselves to?

HOT TIP: If you're going with the buffet, pick foods that can survive in a chafing dish. Take it from me— buffet fish always ends up overcooked. Yucky.

One option that bridges the gap between full service and buffet, and the one we chose for ourselves, is family-style dining. A couple of big platters full of your chosen food come out, and the guests serve themselves as much or as little as they like. It not only cuts back on staff and saves you money but the passing around of platters encourages conversation and community among your guests. Plus, there's often less waste, as people serve themselves what they like. And anything that reminds the guests that, today, you're building a family, is a pretty sweet bonus, I'd say!

4. **ARE YOU INVITING KIDS TO YOUR WEDDING?** If so, this one's for you! Try to negotiate a special meal for the tykes—that will save you the pain of paying the same cost-per-head for them as for adults. Some venues or caterers are friendly to the "under 12 eat free" mentality, so use that as your jumping-off point when entering negotiations. If they won't feed the kids gratis, will they make a less expensive kid's meal? Or allow you to order in pizzas for the young 'uns? Stick them all at the same table, cover it in white paper, throw down some markers and stickers to keep them occupied, and your chances of toasts free from child interruption have just gotten much better!

5. **HOW DO YOU PLAN TO MEET THEIR NEEDS?** Everyone's got different dietary restrictions or predilections, and while you can't please everybody all the time, you can be mindful of how popular the vegetarian/vegan and gluten-free movements have become. Be sure to arrange a special option for those two diets, at the very least, because I have never once been to a dinner party where everyone could eat everything offered. Hippies need to eat, too, people!

6. **CONSIDER YOUR GUESTS' DIGESTIVE RESPONSE.** Bear with me here, but give your grub a second thought. If you're serving gas-inducing foods, or very heavy meals, it can cause discomfort and sluggishness, which might inhibit the guests' likelihood of dancing or sticking around. So if a hardy partying dance-a-thon is high on your list of priorities,

consider serving lighter fare that's less likely to drag your guests down. Refried beans? Maybe not so much.

TOP FIVE DRASTIC, COST-CUTTING STRATEGIES FOR RECEPTION MEALS

1. **IN GENERAL, LESS MEAT = LESS MONEY.** Surf and turf will run you beaucoup bucks, and chicken could certainly save you a bundle, but my favorite option is to go veg! You can easily serve a heavily vegetarian meal to your friends and family without anyone dying of starvation. If you can't imagine a meal without meat, limit it to appetizers and focus on something vegetarian for entrées. There are a million delicious, hearty, and filling options in the veggie world, so don't be afraid to explore and see the savings add up!

   BONUS: It's much better for the environment. So you're killing (or should I say *saving*) two birds with one stone!

2. **THINK OUTSIDE OF THE BOX.** Or, rather, inside the basket. Picnic weddings are picking up speed, and it can cut costs considerably for you. Not just on food, but on rentals, too. No need for chairs, tables, plates, silver, or waitstaff. Have a great local sandwich shop put together three styles of 'wich and side salads with dressing in take-out containers, grab kettle-style chips and cookies in bulk, and create cute, individually boxed meals. With kraft boxes and twine, you can dress up a simple meal display in a jiff! Ask friends and family to lend you blankets for the picnic, craft some throw pillows to toss around, and let your guests choose where to sit. If floor seating is just a little too casual for you, look into renting picnic tables.

   And if sandwiches don't sing your song, try fried chicken boxes. A leg and a breast alongside a biscuit and a container of potato or corn salad would be great at a Southern-themed bash.

3. **FOOD TRUCKS ARE YOUR FRIENDS.** In almost every city across the United States, the mobile cuisine industry is booming. Trucks producing foods of every ethnicity and style are showing up daily, and the quality of some of their treats is on a par with gourmet restaurants. You can hire a food truck to offer the full menu on an all-you-can-eat basis, or negotiate a smaller, limited offering. It's a highly competitive industry, so you might see bigger savings than a traditional caterer can offer. We found an independent taco cart on Craigslist, hired them to cater our engagement party at a ridiculously reasonable rate, and my, what a fiesta we had!

4. **LEAN ON YOUR COMMUNITY.** DIY the food by having a potluck reception, inviting each family to contribute a dish. Or build a cavalcade of family and friends to cook a big meal, such as spaghetti or baked lasagna, on the morning of the wedding. My friend and fellow blogger Daffodil Campbell at Adventures in Paradise once fed forty people for $3 each, and has generously allowed us to include that dinner on page 238! Set up a few barbecues on the lawn, and hire a personal chef to be grill

master for a few hours, with buffet-style toppings, potato salad, chips, green salad, or other DIY-the-day-before side dishes. Your crew will be thrilled to help, it will save you loads of money, and the memory of a kitchen bustling with your near and dear, preparing a feast for your fête, will warm your heart for years to come.

5. **GIVE THEM THE ROYAL TREATMENT.** Serve a British high tea consisting of crustless finger sandwiches (cucumber or smoked salmon, cream cheese, and dill; avocado and arugula; egg and/or tuna salad; ham and pickle), scones or crumpets with clotted cream and jam, and various mini pastries or tarts. This is especially lovely for an afternoon reception, and serving simpler foods lends a fancier feel and keeps costs way down to a minimum!

your booze can't lose

Unless you have high personal convictions about sobriety or teetotaling, providing adult refreshments for your guests can enhance the "party" feel. The unfortunate bummer is that alcohol can put a big dent in your budget if you're not careful. Lots of couples get overwhelmed and feel that their only alternatives to a full bar are to forgo the booze or have a cash bar instead. While there's nothing technically wrong with a cash bar, an open bar goes a long, *long* way in your guests' appreciation. Like food, your venue may require that you use their services, or have strict rules about how the bar is managed, but if they're flexible and open to negotiation, there are plenty of ways to keep the drinks flowing all night while securing your budget.

PUTTING THE BAR IN BARGAIN

- **BYOB.** If you can bring in your own alcohol, there are a few variations on that theme to mull over. Is stocking a full bar at your local warehouse superstore outside your budget? That's okay, friend.

Keeping Your Booze Budget Under Control

1 Don't be afraid to create a diversion. Relabel your Two-Buck Chuck wine with cute personalized labels and no one will be the wiser! You can find loads of download-able templates online. Just Google "free wine label template." In fact, I'm such a nice lady, I've included instructions for relabeling wine bottles in Chapter 9!

2 *Pssst.* If you're serving the *really* cheap stuff—so cheap that you worry that the flavor might be less than lip-smacking—mask that wine by using it to mix up a big batch of sangria (see page 225) or offer squeezes of citrus to brighten that beer.

3 Having a lunch or brunch wedding? It's mimosa time, y'all! Or offer a secondary option of the (much beloved by me) Bloody Mary bar. Mix it up ahead of time, and let your guests create their own garnish skewers by offering celery sticks, olives, cheese cubes, pickles, cherry tomatoes, cooked bacon (!), or defrosted peel-and-eat shrimp! Don't forget the lemon and lime wedges, and a fat bottle of Sriracha if they want to spice it up!

4 Some beverage superstores, such as BevMo! and Binny's Beverage Depot, allow you to return unopened liquor and wine after your event, which eliminates the risk that you'll buy too much and be stuck with tons of leftovers. Just don't buy too little!

5 You're never too old or too classy for Jell-O shots. Cure your Jell-O in a baking pan rather than in cups, cut it into cubes, and skewer them for a more grown-up twist. At MarthaStewart.com, I once saw a gorgeous silver dish full of elegant-looking Champagne-spiked Jell-O served with Chantilly cream. No lie.

6 Do you have an interest in home brew and enough lead time? Get a kit and craft your own signature ale!

7 Hire a bartender, do self-service, or ask a friend to tend. Or rotate tending friends an hour at a time. It's up to you!

- **Pare it back.** Narrow your selection to just beer and wine, whether you use what the venue has in stock, BYO and serve craft brews in bottles, or order a keg of Pabst Blue Ribbon.

- **Offer a signature cocktail.** If beer and wine is too simple for your tastes, add a signature cocktail to the menu—or two of them, one representing each of you. Or make *that* cocktail the only thing you offer. Mix up a big batch ahead of time,

a primer for calculating how much booze to buy

There are plenty of alcohol calculators online that can dispel the "how much will I need" confusion. But if, by the time you read this, society has gone completely off the grid, or you live in a cabin in the woods without Wi-Fi, or your Internet is just plain on the fritz, this equation will give you a starting point:

 # guests × estimated # of drinks they'll drink = total # of drinks needed

Keep these five tips in mind:

1. There are roughly 5 servings of wine and 16 servings of liquor in a 750-milliliter bottle. Divide your total milliliters by these numbers to estimate how many bottles you'll need.

2. Think in terms of a half-bottle of wine per person.

3. In the mixer category, estimate roughly 1 liter of soda, juice, or tonic for every three guests.

4. In the United States, beer kegs generally come in quarter- and half-barrel sizes, which serve about 100 or 200 10-ounce drinks, respectively.

5. And don't forget the ice! Roughly 1.5 pounds per person should do ya.

You're welcome!

or let whoever tends your bar mix them to order. Give the drinks a cute, theme-y name, and stick to just one or two types of liquor. In fact, I'm such a nice lady, I've included a couple sample drink recipes for you on pages 225–27.

HOT TIP: This is another opportunity to extend your theme into the details. Margaritas for your Mexican Fiesta. Mulled wine or spiked cider for a Winter Wonderland. Or play into your location by highlighting a signature cocktail of the region—mint juleps in the land of bourbon, for instance.

decoding the venue-hosted bar

If your venue strictly enforces that you use their bar service, there are usually two ways they charge for it:

1. An open bar for X number of hours for a flat fee, no matter how much or little gets ordered

2. An open bar for X number of hours, at the end of which they tally the total number of drinks as if it were a normal bar and bill you for that at the end of the night

Option 1 is best for you if your guest list is known for their boozy appetites, or if you suspect that might be the case. Option 2 is best for you if your guest list includes mostly light drinkers or nondrinkers, with a few outliers here and there.

Whichever option you select, try negotiating a limited offering there as well. Would they allow you to offer just wine and beer and/or a signature cocktail? Or, keep the bar open for cocktail hour, then cut it down to wine service once dinner is served?

When you calculate the number of hours you'll need, don't be afraid to cut the alcohol flow an hour before your wedding officially ends. It'll help people sober up and keep your costs down by just that much more.

champagne schlampagne

Yeah, yeah . . . it's traditional to toast with Champagne (or its cheaper cousin, Prosecco) at weddings. But honestly, at every event I go to, I hear more people turn down the bubbly in favor of another type of drink. "It goes straight to my head," they say. "It gives me the worst hangovers," they say. *I'm* even picky about drinking bubbly at events because, in my opinion, cheap bubbly is worse than cheap wine or beer.

HINT: If your budget allows for only the cheapest of champers, grab some strawberry puree at your grocer and put a teaspoon in the bottom of each glass to sweeten it and add a romantic red hue.

If you order enough for each guest to have a flute, I promise that a great deal of that, along with your money, is going down the drain. Save yourself the trouble and cash by omitting it altogether, or having a handful of bottles for anyone who requests it.

If you simply cannot picture your wedding without Champagne, buy from a retailer who allows unopened returns, and have the staff ask each guest if he or she wants some for the toast rather than autopouring. That way you can recoup some costs if your guests aren't big bubbly fans.

I Had to See It to Believe It!

My sister had a brilliant idea for her beachy bash. She served virgin, "pour your own" punch in a big bowl, and left several bottles of spiced rum nearby for guests to spike their drinks, if they so desired. I loved this idea because it had a "something for everyone" mentality that saved her and her hubby a bundle of money!

—**Dana**

Remember Brittany from Chapter 4—our two-time bride after her officiant oopsie? She and her husband taste-tested several brands of boxed wine until they found the most palatable blends available and served them "help yourself" style, along with her father's home-brewed mead, at her fabulous wedding. It was all delicious and got the job done for very little scratch.

My girlfriend Megan and her husband are craft beer aficionados, and thus very friendly with an amazing local artisanal brewing company, who hooked them up with tons of their signature bevvies for a super-reasonable price because of their good relationship and ongoing patronage. Are there local breweries or wineries you've become cozy with and would they be willing to work out a bulk deal?

a cake by any other name

The wedding cake is a quintessential part of traditional weddings. The ritual of cutting it is significant because it's the first task a couple undertakes as newlyweds. The good news: You can apply that concept to any other dessert that speaks to you, if cake doesn't make your mouth water. But we'll get to that soon enough.

Traditional wedding cakes can rack up a high cost per slice, but don't let that scare you away just yet. Consider the following:

- You can go the fakey-cakey route by having a dummy cake (Styrofoam rounds, iced and decorated) with only one real tier, or just a secret compartment in the lowest tier, to give you and your honey something to actually put a knife through. Then have a plain (and much less expensive) sheet cake in the back that's used for serving your guests.
- I've heard great things about certain grocery store and Costco wedding cakes. Don't let the fact that they come from somewhere other than a bridal bakery throw you.
- Cupcakes have recently experienced a huge surge in popularity at weddings. Type "cupcake" into Pinterest and charming cuppie displays abound. They're a nice option because you can offer a variety of flavors rather than just one or two, and guests can help themselves, eliminating the need for service, plates, and forks.
- If you simply must have a whole, real, decorated cake, choose simple design elements to keep the cost down. Go

with fewer tiers (and supplement with hidden sheet cake, if necessary), real flowers instead of sugar flowers, decoration on only one layer, simple flavors, common shapes, and bring your own topper.

Whichever method of cake delivery you choose, your guests don't need huge slices. If you think some people will want more, put a small table with extra slices out after dessert for guests to help themselves.

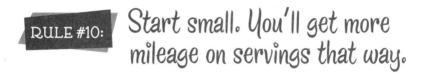

RULE #10: *Start small. You'll get more mileage on servings that way.*

alternative desserts: when cake doesn't cut it

There is no rule that says you must serve cake, so if you've got an open mind or specific favorite, feel free to express yourself and serve that instead! Neither Hunter nor I are huge cake people, but we fell in love with a specific cream puff made here in Los Angeles. We arranged for the bakery to come and fill the puffs onsite, to order, which kept them from getting soggy and sad. Rather than cutting the cake, we smashed the cream puff—a very fun, and yummy, twist on tradition.

SOME FAVORITE DESSERT ALTERNATIVES

- **Pies:** Especially great if your region is known for a specific type of fruit.

- **Double-duty opportunity:** Use pies, or mini-cakes, as centerpieces that double up as dessert once dinner's said and done. Or, set up a candy buffet with bulk treats from a local sweet shop that can double as favors. Glassine bags and twist ties are all you need so guests can scoop their favorite blend of sugary treats. Be sure to complement the season when possible—who doesn't love Cadbury Eggs or Peeps in the springtime, or candy corn in the fall?

- **A sundae bar:** A few flavors of ice cream and tasty topping choices will leave your guests gooey with childhood nostalgia. Have a bunch of big cookies nearby if they would rather make ice cream sandwiches!

- **A s'mores bar:** Cans of Sterno nestled in a pebble-filled planter box can substitute for a campfire on any tabletop. Provide skewers alongside an assortment of graham crackers, marshmallows, and various tasty chocolate bars to let your guests customize their own sweet treats.

- **Cotton candy:** You can rent a cotton candy machine for surprisingly low cost, and spin your guests a sweet dessert on a stick.

  HOT TIP: Spin the sugar onto colored glowsticks for a fabulously funky twist! Google will reveal its magic if you simply cannot picture what I mean.

- **Macarons:** Another dessert treat experiencing a worthy surge in popularity, these light-as-air, crunchy, cream-filled sandwich-cookie-like treats are an elegant and festive alternative that will leave your guests licking their lips.

The following four options can be displayed in stacked tiers to resemble cake, for an unexpected twist on an old tradition:

1. COOKIES: Serve them with shot glasses of milk or coffee to add another special touch. Oreos look great like this, if you're having a black-and-white wedding.

   HOT TIP: Hit up your favorite local bakery or cookie shop for deep discounts on day-old cookies that taste just as good as new. Los Angeles's iconic Diddy Riese cookies are only 35 cents each, and a day-old dozen costs a measly $1.50!

2. **DONUTS**: Because "mmmm, donuts" is a universal language. Caterers and restaurants could whip up fresh donuts as part of your package (there's nothing like 'em), or you can hire in a "fry girl" to come hook up your guests. I've always been partial to Krispy Kreme. Talk to your local shop and see if they'd be willing to do a delivery of "hot now" donuts to your event in time for dessert!

3. **RICE KRISPIE TREATS**: Make these ahead in square pans tapering in size, and stack them to create a "cake" that will have your guests oohing and aahing over its creativity. For a colorful twist, follow the same recipe, but use Fruity Pebbles or Cocoa Puffs. To dress it up, tie ribbon around one of the tiers or garnish with fruit.

4. **CHEESE SELECTION**: A valid alternative to the dessert course by French standards. Stack three lovely cheese wheels in the shape of a tiered cake, and have a unique dessert that's as savory as it is sassy.

9 | Down the rabbit hole of possibilities

DIY projects for dummies

DIY or Die

THE CULT OF CRAFTING

In case you've been living under a rock, let me clarify this chapter's title. DIY stands for "do it yourself." Which, in the case of most weddings, actually should be GOTDIFY (get others to do it for you). That's because:

1. Not everyone was born with the Martha Stewart gene, yet handcrafted elements are extremely popular in the world of wedding decor. Because they feel, well . . . handmade. Like, *love* went into making them.

2. You're most likely working with a shortage of free time. And if you're anything like the majority of craft-mesmerized ladies I know, your eyes are bigger than your proverbial stomach and you'll overestimate what you can reasonably accomplish in the amount of time you have. Instead, overestimate the time that will go into any project you undertake. You'll need it, along with some help.

3. You will (and I promise you this, so pay attention), you *will* find yourself on the floor of your living room, at 2:53 in the morning, covered in glitter and hot-glue-gun burns, having just unwittingly affixed your finger to the paper flower you were constructing (and if you're like me, halfway through a bottle of wine), *sobbing uncontrollably* and begging your fiancé for a simple courthouse elopement. Because all of a sudden, your wedding (but really just your craft ambition) is way bigger than you can handle. Honey, this will likely happen more than once, so do us both a favor and gird your loins now, okay?

4. You probably have one, or a few, stupidly talented, artsy-crafty friends or family members in your crew, so use them. You will not be inducted into some secret bridal craft-goddess sorority for handcrafting your entire wedding totally solo. Let's be real: they sell deliberately made-to-look-handmade decor items at major craft chains. Lean on your people now, and forever maintain your sanity.

5. There are literally thousands of people out there who love to craft, and they are excellent at it and would love nothing more than to do it for you—for a fee, that is. However, to determine if it's worth the investment, consider the value of your time and the supplies you'll need to accomplish any project you contemplate undertaking. Oftentimes the machines, pieces, parts, and various other sundry "ingredients" you'll need for your craft, *plus the amount of your time it will eat up,* may cost more than just buying it from someone on Etsy.

RULE #11: Do not hold yourself to Martha Stewart standards if crafting isn't in your blood.

down the rabbit hole of possibilities

Read enough books and blogs, or spend enough time on Pinterest, and you'll discover that there seems to be no end to the gadgets and gizmos, materials and supplies that can be used to craft pretty much every element of your wedding. Here's a peek at the most commonly used items.

A PRIMER ON CRAFTING MATERIALS (FOR THOSE OF YOU WHO'VE YET TO MASTER A GLUE GUN)

- Paper: scrapbook prints, metallic, crepe, cardstock, kraft, matte, seeded, natural, etc.
- Writing instruments: pens, pencils, markers, calligraphy tools
- Paper punches
- Rubber stamps
- Embossers
- Adhesives: glue, glue dots, hot glue, spray glue, tape, Mod Podge, staplers, fusible bonding, etc.

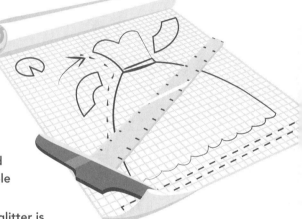

- Glitter! (But beware: glitter is the herpes of crafting. Once you get it, you can't seem to get rid of it.)
- Cutting tools: X-acto knives, straight scissors, decorative scissors, pinking shears, rotary knife, trimmers, etc.
- Ribbon, twine, or decorative washi tape
- Rulers
- Fabric: felt, burlap, muslin, cotton, organza, tulle, lace, wool, gingham, etc.
- Wire: fishing line, fine-gauge, thick-gauge, pipe cleaners, etc.
- Wine: for your sanity

- Paint: acrylic, watercolor, fabric, puffy, wood, stain, sealant, etc.
- Brushes
- Stickers
- Glassware: vases, votive holders, jars, bottles, bowls, flutes, candlesticks, mirrors, etc.
- Ephemera: buttons, rhinestones, crystals, poms, beads, moss, rocks, etc.

And then there are the machines, like the Cricut, the Gocco, button makers, die cutters, screen printers, adhesive backers, sewing machines, sergers, and more. But this is for all super-hardcore crafting addicts. Stick to the gateway drugs for now, young grasshopper.

DIY does not stand for . . .

"Duplicate it yourself." Sure, imitation is the sincerest form of flattery, but keep in mind that someone's own creativity, talents, and time went into creating the object of your desire, and thus it is that person's intellectual property. Sure, you can use it as *inspiration* for your own project, but handing a picture of someone else's work to an artisan and asking to have it duplicated for your own use is kinda shady and should be avoided.

Alternatively, it is acceptable to present a photo or two to your florist, graphic designer, or other, and say, "Here's what I love about this. Could you take inspiration from these to make something new for me?"

And lastly, I am sure most of you have more common sense than this, but as your sensei of wedding knowledge, I implore you: should you find yourself to be very crafty, and wish to make a few dollars from your talents, please *do not ever* copy someone else's work and sell it as your own on Etsy. Thanks.

DIY projects for dummies

So because I am nothing, if not an enabler, I am going to big-sister you into your addiction by sharing with you some of my most favorite DIY projects. Try one, if you dare! Mwahahahaha!

I'm admittedly not the craftiest beaver in the creek, but I whole-heartedly recognize both the monetary and the sentimental value of using your imagination, hands, and heart to create whatever elements possible for your wedding (or life)—or at least having helpful, craftier beavers lend a hand to get 'er done! In that vein, I've cultivated some of my most affordable, least-crafty, person-friendly projects that can make the biggest impact on your wedding design. Let's hope they'll lend you the rush of endorphins that comes with the "I made this!" moment of crafting rather than the "Lord, help me, I give up" desperate uncorking of your second bottle of wine with your teeth like a rabid animal.

For what it's worth, you can find video tutorials to support some of these crafts, and a couple others (while affording you plentiful opportunities to laugh at Hunter and me nerding out *big time*) on my YouTube channel, http://youtube.com/brokeassbride.

DIY
1 The Mighty Mason Jar

This is the workhorse of wedding crafting. Inexpensive, available in a multitude of shapes and sizes, and easy to find used. Mason jars can hold beverages, act as decor or centerpieces, and do a whole lot more! What's even better than buying Masons for your wedding? Save every olive, pickle, jam, and salsa jar (and ask your family and friends to do the same) for the period leading up to your wedding, and recycle these freebies at your wedding! Or buy up a former bride's bounty on a resale site. Here is a sampling of my favorite ways you can incorporate the mighty Mason jar into your DIY wedding plans.

AS VASES

Painted neon, metallic, or any color: Coat the inside with acrylic/water-based paint so the exterior glass can provide a naturally shinier finish. (But if you're going to use them as vases, place a plastic cup inside to put the water in or else it will peel the paint.) Or paint the outside of the jar if you prefer a matte look.

Painted with chalkboard paint: Do the outside if you go this route.

Planters: Plant flowers, succulents, or herbs in advance, using potting soil and/or pebbles or moss to finish.

Countrified: Wrap them with burlap, doilies, and twine.

Terrariums: For a surprising twist, place little figurines of people, animals, or dinosaurs within or around your plants!

Hanging vases: Dangle them from tree branches or along a clothesline. Wrap thin-gauge wire tightly around the neck of the jar, and wrap it around the clothesline for a secure hang.

Like a regular old vase: Line the inside of the jar with a banana leaf for a great way to hide the stems naturally.

Submerged flowers in water: They are beautiful on their own or with a floating candle on top. Choose flowers with hearty petals that can stand up to a good soaking.

Glittered: Mod Podge is magical stuff, yo. Just mix your glitter into the Mod Podge and paint it however you like it! For thicker glitter action, do multiple coats. Again, coat the inside for a shiny outer look, or paint the outside if you'd prefer more texture.

Mod Podged: Use an interestingly printed paper, such as sheet music, comic books, or literature, and use Mod Podge as both your base glue and top coat.

Tinted: Mix food coloring with Mod Podge and paint it in layers on the inside of your jar to create a colored, transparent hue.

AS SOURCES OF LIGHT

Candle-fied: Fill with citronella oil and give it a wick, pour with wax, or drop simple votives inside.

Lantern-ified: Sprayed with frosted-glass paint and lit from within, this looks really cool. It also works great with the tinted and (lightly) glittered versions above.

Silhouette-ified: Place paper silhouette cutouts or stencils on the jars, spray-paint the whole jar, and remove the stencils to let a candle inside illuminate the silhouettes.

Spray-painted: If you do this after wrapping the jar body with ribbon, or other uneven covering like lace or doilies, leaving gaps for the paint, when you remove the cover it will reveal graphic designs through which light can shine.

AS DECOR

Fairy dust jars: Cut a glowstick and flick the contents into your jar. Add diamond glitter and shake!

Filled with olive oil and old photos: Using black and white gives the photos a fancy sepia effect.

Filled with found objects: Buttons, marbles, jelly beans, spools of thread, coffee beans, nuts, fabric poms, coins, or other bric-a-brac.

As a still life: Create dioramas inside with action figures or dolls. This works best if you lay the jar on its side.

Snow globes: Glue a figure or statue to the inside of your lid, fill the jar with water and glitter, and screw the lid on tightly. Stand the jar on its head, and encourage guests to shake for effect. Using a thicker base, like castor oil, sustains the magic by slowing the rate at which the glitter settles.

2 Custom Tablecloths, Runners, or Napkins

These are real money-savers compared with renting linens from a company. The fabrics suggested can be affordably sourced at your local craft or hobby supply (especially if you keep a keen eye out for coupons and sales!).

SUPPLIES

ruler or measuring tape	**fabric**
chalk	**pinking shears**

1. Measure your table, and determine the desired length of fabric overhang. For napkins, decide on a shape, and determine the measurements. Napkins are generally 12, 14, or 16 inches square. For runners, measure them to be about one-third the width of your table.

2. Chalk out the measurements on your fabric surface.

3. Cut along your lines using pinking shears. (Why pinking shears? The zigzag trim helps prevent fraying and eliminates the need for hemming.) Or, for a more "finished" look without noodling around with needles, cut with fabric scissors and use no-sew fusible bonding to fold, iron, and voilà! Faux-hemmed clean edges.

HINT: Use twine to tie rocks into the corners of your cloths to weight them down if your reception might encounter an unexpected breeze.

BONUS TIP: Iron freezer paper onto fabric to adhere and reinforce it, cut it all down to 8 ½ x 11 inches, and you can print directly onto the fabric! Remove the freezer paper afterward, and do with the printed fabric what you will! Using spray adhesive, you can appliqué great designs or place mats onto a plain muslin tablecloth for beautiful enhancements.

ALTERNATIVE TABLE COVERING IDEA FOR MORE CASUAL AFFAIRS: Measure the tables' surfaces and cut kraft paper to fit. Affix the paper to the corners with glue dots, and decorate the surface with rubber stamps, draw place-setting stencils, or write your guests' names at their designated seats. Toss markers or crayons into jars and let your guests doodle while they dine!

Suggested Uses

- Decorate natural muslin, canvas, or burlap (available most inexpensively at Home Depot) with rubber stamps and accent with bright napkins.

- Use a relevant pattern such as gingham for a rustic picnic or European feel, or damask for an upscale elegance.

- Use spray adhesive to apply decorative trim, such as lace or geometric shapes cut from contrasting fabrics.

DIY Pimp Cups

Blingy goblets are a terrific way for you and your new spouse, or entire bridal party (did someone say "rehearsal dinner gifts?"), to celebrate with at the wedding and also have as a keepsake reminder of the big day as long as your glassware shall live! I surprised Hunter with a pair that said "Hubby" and "Wifey" at our place settings at the reception, but doing it yourself is a much cheaper and more customized approach!

HINT: Have a "make-your-own" craft session at your bachelor/-ette party.

SUPPLIES

large round goblets (check your dollar store for these!)

newspaper (optional)

nontoxic spray paint (optional)

rhinestones

Super Glue

food-grade Mod Podge

1. If you wish to spray-paint the cups, turn them upside down on newspaper and apply several light coats of paint to the outside, allowing them to dry thoroughly in between.

   HINT: Black or gold look extra crunk!

2. Apply rhinestones with Super Glue, being careful to just use a tiny drop for each stone to avoid seepage around the edges.

3. Once dry, seal with a thin coat of food-grade Mod Podge all over the outside and lip of the cup, and allow it to dry. Cheers, homey!

DIY 4   Tie-Dyed Paper

A terrifically fun "messy craft," this paper can be used as backing on invitations or signage at the wedding/reception, or use craft punches to create shapes and adhere them to adorn plain paper or wood signage. This also makes a great background for hanging pennant banners, linked with string.

SUPPLIES

shaving cream

rimmed baking sheet

food coloring

rubber gloves

blank paper (recycled preferred)

old washcloths or scrap fabric

drying rack

1. Spray a layer of shaving cream over the bottom of the baking sheet.

2. Add several drops of food coloring to the cream. Use more for bolder, vibrant colors; use less for softer pastels. Suggested combinations are red and yellow, blue and green.

3. Using a gloved hand, swirl the cream around until the colors are spread through in a way that pleases you. Don't blend it completely, leave darker swirls here and there. Add more food coloring, if needed.

4. Gently place the blank paper on top of the shaving cream, patting it down to ensure even coverage.

5. Lift the paper off, and wipe off the excess cream with a towel. Peep that sweet design you just created!

6. Set on the rack to dry.

DIY 5 — Instant Chalkboard Signage and Decor

Chalkboard displays are perfectly multifaceted for varied uses at a wedding. Possible incarnations include signage at the wedding (welcome sign, menu, table numbers/names), decor, centerpiece vases, wood boards, your ceremony backdrop—the sky's the limit!

SUPPLIES

- Any item you wish to create a chalkboard surface on (wood, trays, vases, plates, etc.)
- masking tape
- primer
- sponge roller or sponge paintbrush
- chalkboard paint
- chalk
- cloth

1. If you wish to paint only a specific area of the surface, tape off that area and prime it.

2. Apply a thin layer of chalkboard paint. Allow it to dry. Repeat, taking care to get full, even coverage. Allow it to dry completely.

3. Condition it by rubbing the side of a piece of chalk over the whole surface. This helps with future erasing and prevents drawings from leaving permanent marks.

4. Wipe gently clean with a lightly damp cloth to remove the conditioning chalk. Allow to dry.

Write the couple a message!

DIY 6 Custom Chalkboard Paint Color

If the customary black or green chalkboard colors don't suit your style, you can turn any hue of paint into a chalk-friendly surface with this easy hack!

SUPPLIES

flat-finish latex paint in any color

container

unsanded tile grout

stirrer

roller or sponge paintbrush

150-grit sandpaper

chalk

cloth

1. Pour 1 cup of paint into a large container.

2. Add 2 tablespoons of unsanded tile grout.

3. Mix with a paint stirrer, carefully breaking up clumps.

4. Apply paint with a roller or a sponge paintbrush to a primed or painted surface. Allow to dry. Repeat, taking care to get full, even coverage. Allow to dry.

5. Smooth the area with sandpaper, and wipe off the dust.

6. Condition by rubbing the side of a piece of chalk over the whole surface. Wipe clean gently with a lightly damp cloth. Allow to dry.

DIY 7 Relabeled Wine Bottles

Disguise inexpensive table wine bottles (did someone say Two-Buck Chuck?) at the bar, as centerpiece elements, include in basket-style centerpieces (see page 61), or use the bottles as table numbers (see page 61), and let guests imbibe their delicious contents during dinner service.

SUPPLIES

wine bottles

sink or soaking tub

water

sponge

downloadable templates (the Internet shares its bounty, folks!)

label paper (or regular paper and spray adhesive)

printer

scissors

1. Soak your bottles overnight in a sink or tub to loosen the labels. Peel them off with your fingers and use the sponge to remove excess residue. Allow to dry completely.

2. Lay out your design using downloadable templates, and print out.

3. Cut the label down to size and affix to the bottle, adding adhesives, if necessary.

4. Allow to dry and admire your handiwork!

Repotted Succulents

Display these as eco-friendly centerpieces, give them as favors (see page 61), have bridesmaids carry them down the aisle in lieu of bouquets, or use them as scattered decor on your escort card table, the bar.

SUPPLIES

succulent cuttings

pots (glass vases, bowls, wood boxes, baskets, votives, terra-cotta pots, or hollowed-out gourds)

potting soil

stones, gravel, or moss (optional)

1. Let your succulent cuttings sit out overnight to allow the "nub," where it was cut, to dry out and harden a bit.

2. Fill your vessel of choice with potting soil, then bury the nub in the soil, packing it around the clipping to help it stand up. If using different types of succulent, vary their size and height for visual interest.

3. Top the potting soil with tiny stones, gravel, or moss, if you wish.

   HOT TIP: To replant after the event, follow the same steps, and plant wherever you like!

DIY

9 Dessert Pedestals

These make beautiful cake stands, dessert displays, or center-piece risers.

SUPPLIES

cups, bowls, candlesticks (which work best), or sturdy, thick stemware for the base/risers (antique or vintage, thrifted items preferred)

1 or more plates or platters for the top of the pedestal

Super Glue

something to weight the pedestal down while drying

1. Using your choice of overturned cup, bowl, or candlestick for the base, mix and match with your platters to find a good fit in terms of visual appeal, height, and balance.

2. Apply a thin layer of Super Glue to the rim of the surface that you'll connect to the bottom of your platter, and set the platter on top.

3. Set your weight on the center of the surface to apply constant pressure while it dries. Use care not to apply too much weight and break your items.

4. If you like, add a smaller tier or two above the first tier by repeating steps 1–3, taking care to maintain balanced centering.

> HINT: Add a small plate or saucer under narrower bases like candlesticks or teacups for extra stability.

Advice from the Craftily Challenged

COUPLE:
Mallory Murphy Viscardi and James Viscardi

LOCATION:
Long Island, New York

BUDGET: *$15,000*

. . . .

"The first time I tried crafting—real crafting, not just crafts I intended to gift to my mother—I glued my whole hand to my desk with Super Glue. Twice. Any sensible woman would have called it quits (and let someone else in her group finish the model for the Marketing presentation), but I've never claimed to be sensible. It's probably this disconnect from sensibility that caused me to declare that my wedding would be 'handmade.' I'm creative enough, I reasoned, and a fast learner. (Translation: I'm a terribly stubborn perfectionist.)

"If I had to pick just one piece of advice to send to brides-to-be that are considering handcrafting their wedding, it would be this: step up to the plate and do it. You'll fail a little at first, but you know what? Experience and trial and error will soon replace the doubt you feel now; and I promise you, the feeling that will wash over you when you see your guests marvel at the beautiful setting you created just for them to enjoy makes it all worth it. (And keep acetone, or nail polish remover, on hand. It dissolves Super Glue, in case you find yourself glued to a piece of furniture in your trial-and-error phase.) " **—MALLORY**

Save Green, Be Green

Weddings have a big-ass impact on the environment. More than you'd imagine, I'll wager. The travel, transport, paper products, fresh flowers, food, decor, honeymoon, and more each generate some form of waste, whether it be carbon, trash, electronic, or otherwise. Did you know that your wedding can generate almost as much carbon waste (14.5 tons) as you do just living normally for a year (17.1 tons)? Pretty shocking considering that your wedding lasts a day or at most a few!

In light of our ongoing environmental turmoil, it makes us all better humans when we step up and take responsibility for our piece in the eco-puzzle, and the best way to start (or improve on your already green outlook) is to do whatever you can to make your wedding as environmentally conscious as possible. Here's the bonus: you'll be kicking off your new life together on the right foot, with all kinds of good karma for your eco-mindedness!

something old, something new, something borrowed, something ... green?

There are tons of ways to minimize the footprint of your fête, but you'll quickly find that many companies (sadly) charge quite a premium for their "eco" products and services. Ah, yes, the dreaded "green tax." Fear not, young friend! There are plenty of affordable, or even money-saving, options, from biodegradable disposables to vintage and handmade alternatives.

THE BIGGEST CARBON CULPRITS

1. Travel
2. Waste
3. Fresh flowers
4. Paper
5. Food

Let's break down each one and consider some eco-friendlier options, along with some pitfalls to avoid.

TRAVEL

Peeps are going to have to get to your wedding. This can involve any mode of transport, from trains to planes to automobiles. Heck, depending on your plans, you might even need a plane to get to your own wedding. Travel = carbon. Beyond that, if your ceremony and reception aren't in the same place, there's travel between the two to consider. And then back home, or to the hotel, or to the airport, and the carbon repeats.

Cut it back, Jack! Here are four tips:

1. You can easily shave down the travel by having your wedding in a location central to where most of your guests reside (if such a place exists).

2. Try to keep your ceremony and reception locations together, or as close together, as possible.

3. Encourage your guests to use public transit or to carpool.

4. Consider buying carbon offset credits in lieu of giving favors at the end of the night. You can include a note at each place setting, or in your program, stating that you've done so. And, let's be real: favors often get left behind or thrown away anyway. This way your expense goes toward something good!

WASTE

Speaking of favors being thrown away, the amount of trash a wedding can generate is mind-boggling. Like, 400 to 600 pounds of trash mind-boggling! Yes, for just one event. Awoooooooga! You can control the amount of waste you generate by reusing what you can or recycling as much as possible after the wedding. But also, one person's trash is another bride's treasure, so don't forget to "pre-cycle" as much as you can by buying used materials through Craigslist, online message boards, flea markets, estate sales, and the like.

Here are four tips for trashing waste:

1. Rather than throwing your leftover food and cake away at the end of the night, arrange for your caterer (or a trusted friend/family member) to drop it off with a local shelter or program that will get it to people in need.

2. Choose recycled materials whenever possible, such as paper, mismatched vintage flatware and dishes, and remnants of fabric. Stamps, decoupage, paint, and trim can make anything old seem new again!

3. If you must go disposable, opt for more eco-friendly alternatives, such as corn-based plastic flatware and dishes.

4. Get your "something borrowed" on. Rather than buying new jewelry with which to accessorize, borrow pieces from friends or family and breathe new life into heirlooms.

FRESH FLOWERS

Weddings and blooms are inextricably linked—but the environment can bear a surprising burden for their beauty. Here are my five top tips for cutting back on that impact!

1. A fixation on specific blooms can be harmful to both your bank account and Mother Earth. Flying in specific (pesticide-coated) flowers from around the world when they're not locally available is as much an expense of carbon (from the plane) as it is money. *¡No bueno!* Instead, pick a color scheme and let your florist choose local, seasonal flowers that complement your style (or source them yourself at the local floral mart), and you'll save green while being green.

   HOT TIP: Baby's Breath is not just an inexpensive filler for prom corsages anymore! Packed into galvanized tubs or Mason jars, even tied into a bouquet, this oft-overlooked, affordable flower packs a whimsical, romantic punch when used in large quantities.

2. Look beyond the flowers at your farmer's market and pimp out your bouquet or centerpieces with attractive produce for an unexpected, fresh twist! Artichokes, pomegranates, colorful citrus fruits, and grapes make great "spotlight" pieces, while hearty greens such as kale make for a great frame and filler.

3. If you're using fresh florals for the bridal party bouquets, then put them to double-duty as centerpieces for your head table at the reception. Arrange Mason jars or vases on your tabletop, and have your coordinator or a trusted friend drop the bridesmaids' bouquets in them after the ceremony. Voilà! Instant recycled decor! Go one step further by donating the centerpieces to a hospital or nursing home the next day and let your flowers brighten someone else's tomorrow!

4. Consider the alternatives! Nonfloral centerpieces are just as, if not more, beautiful—and often more affordable. Succulents are regenerative and can be replanted (who'd-a-thunk it? Recyclable plants!), and if you live in the right region, you can sneakily score cuttings from your neighborhood to use, rather than buying new. Lucky for you, I'm a nice enough lady that I included instructions for repotting succulent cuttings as centerpieces; see page 157 in Chapter 9!

   HOT TIP: There's almost always someone on Craigslist offloading plants and trimmings for free, so check there, too!

5. If cactus trimmings aren't your jam, opt for an alternative centerpiece option (remember page 61 in Chapter 3?), Why not repurpose regular, scrapbook, or tissue paper to craft your own flowers? Pinterest is teeming with methods to create all manner of paper flowers, and it ups your style quotient to craft them with paper from a used book for literary fiends, sheet music for musicians, or comic books for the graphic-novel lovers among us. Tea-stain it for a rustic look. Dye it for a pop of color. Oh, what's that? How do you dye paper? Turns out, I'm such a nice lady, I've also included instructions for that in Chapter 9 (and it's super simple!).

PAPER

Save-the-dates. Invitations. Response cards. Programs. Menus. Signage. Escort cards. Favor tags. Thank-you notes. Weddings make the paper industry go 'round just as much as the printing companies do, I swear! But you know where all that paper ends up at the end of the big day? The trash. Try this instead:

1. **MAKE MAMA EARTH SMILE.** Reduce your paper usage as much as humanly possible. Send postcards or, better yet, electronic information when you can (see page 42). Skip fancy envelope liners or belly bands. For our invitations, we

Making a Sustainable Start

COUPLE:
Becca and Jason

LOCATION:
Topanga Canyon, California

BUDGET:
roughly $22,500

. . . .

Sustainability issues framed every wedding choice we made, from organic and local catering, to home-planted succulent centerpieces, to our e-mailed save-the-dates and single-page recycled invitations. But the most important green choice we made wasn't any single specific item: it was the upfront decision to focus our wedding day on the marriage and celebration of emotion, instead of focusing on "what a wedding should be" and the "stuff you have to buy." That doesn't mean we didn't have an amazing party (we did), or that we didn't care about the decor (in fact, I went a little bit bonkers with it); but it meant we were able to cut the wedding stuff that didn't matter to us, so we could focus on the fun (a great DJ, for instance).

Because sustainability, simplicity, and emotion framed our wedding, we started with a nature-filled setting that was already beautiful and didn't need much decoration, which helped us design a more casual wedding overall. Our hilltop ceremony needed only white chairs, and for the indoor reception we simply draped some *papel picado* (Mexican wedding flags) and white Christmas lights from the rafters and placed tea lights in Mason jars (repurposed pasta and other food jars we spray-painted with a soft frosted-glass glowy look) around the room.

In the end, my single favorite green choice was to forgo favors. Instead of buying a small throwaway trinket, we got down to the WHY of giving favors (expressing gratitude for the effort people made to join us) and wrote every guest a personalized welcome-to-our-wedding-and-thank-you-for-coming card (on recycled paper, of course) that doubled as their escort cards. The act of writing 150 cards to our wedding guests was a little insane, but it was one of the most powerful and beautiful parts of our wedding. We got to tell everyone exactly how much we loved them and how much it meant that they shared in our wedding day, and everyone started the day with emotion at the forefront.

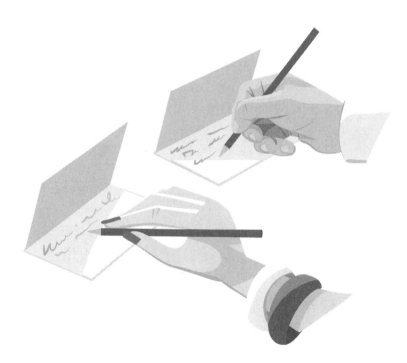

had an artistic friend draw a cartoon of us riding a magic carpet high above the planet. On the reverse, we laid out the details about the big day and directed guests to our wedding website. We printed them at Kinko's and sent them out as small posters, folded and wrapped in vintage sari fabric.

2. **USE RECYCLED PAPER TO BEGIN WITH.** We've already established that it can add mad style to your project! Print with soy ink, if you can. It's less toxic, and more biodegradable than regular ink.

3. **OMIT MENUS OR PROGRAMS IN FAVOR OF DIY CHALKBOARDS!** Oh, snap, I'm even a nice enough lady that I've provided instructions for this crazy-simple, color scheme–tailorable craft in Chapter 9!

FOOD

I've covered the subject of food already, so just reread the "Less meat = less money" portion of Chapter 8, and the subsection on page 163 about waste, and you're golden. Other ways you can up your green game are by serving locally sourced, seasonal, and organic items as much as possible. If you're self-catering, the local farmer's market is a great place to score amazing bulk deals on the greenest goods around. It's almost always easier to haggle if you catch them near closing time. They're more eager to offload the fresh stuff so it doesn't rot in their trucks. And be sure to avoid disposables as much as possible, people!

bride$hare: the carpool lane of wedding planning

My favorite greenifying method by far is to use Bride$hare. "What is Bride$haring?" you ask. Only the best way ever known to save both the earth and money! Well, I think so, but maybe I'm biased. Full disclosure! I did coin the term, after all. Come a little closer, I'll tell you a story . . .

After I first blogged about our wedding venue and our initial design plans, I had more than a few girls contact me who were either already getting married at the same location or were contemplating it. I was happy to connect with all of them, but the most exciting e-mail I received came from a girl named Rebecca Rose.

Rebecca had stumbled across my site one day and fell in love with my color board and theme. As she read further, she realized that we were booked for our receptions at the same venue. She saw a post I had written concerning lighting in the dining area, and she contacted me:

> *It's eerie how many similar ideas we have. Anyway, if you wanted to think about lanterns and maybe other decor, I'd be glad to share costs on things that can be reused. Through work I have a few connections that can get me wholesale prices on some of the stuff. I know you're probably very busy, but let's chat at some time. Maybe we can share some other costs and save some money! I hope you don't think I'm poaching your style too much . . . it's just that you're too cool for school!*

Poaching my style? Girlfriend, please! Now, I do know some brides who are very possessive of their designs and wedding style. I've read countless snarky message-board postings from girls complaining about other brides "biting" their designs. But I was just thrilled to know that someone out there dug it, much less wanted to emulate it!

P.S.: I'll never really get that notion of people stealing other people's style. Especially in weddings, where trends are so prevalently embraced. Yes, we borrow inspiration from one another, especially if it's posted all over the Internet, people! What do you expect? To be clear, I don't condone copycat weddings; but letting another couple's style influence your own is only natural, and no one should be made to feel bad about that.

Over the months of my wedding research, I'd heard of couples sharing the cost of Chiavari chairs, tents, or recycling church flowers over a weekend, but I had never considered this level of sharing and reuse. It's so much smarter and safer than fronting the money yourselves at the start, and then just hoping to recoup costs by reselling these items afterward. It halves the cost and the waste, in one fell swoop!

With all of Hunter's and my efforts to be as eco-conscious as possible during planning, this struck me as an especially fortuitous way to not only save green but also *be* green. Bride$hare: the carpool lane for weddings!

Rebecca and I met several times during the planning process, and it was always so much fun to spend some time with a like-minded bride, planning together for our respective big days. We'd "ooh" and "aah" over color combinations, pick out fun decor elements to share, and inspire each other with ideas. We even co-owned DIY and crafting supplies, buying materials in bulk and trading tools!

"But Dana," you fret, "not everyone has a public forum as you do. How are we expected to find bridal partners?"

Well, my bridal biddies, there are a number of ways!

- The easiest is to ask your venue contact if he or she will put you in touch with the couple(s) booked there over the same weekend, or possibly even the same month or season. On that note . . .

- Ask your vendors to put you in touch with their other clients.
- Never underestimate the magical wonderland of resources that is the Internet. Message boards on your favorite wedding websites are a wonderful place to "meet" other engaged peeps, and most sites have local boards and "month twin" areas where you can find potential buddies or try searching for similar themes or color choices. Check out the Resources on page 246 for more of my favorite websites.

You never know how eager other folks might be to upgrade their plans for a downgrade in cost. Especially those of you with more common color schemes: you Tiffany blue and chocolate browners; you black, white, and silver types; you yellow and gray fanatics; you "blush and bashful" dames and blokes. You know you're out there. Go . . . find one another!

shareable wares

What you share beforehand or recycle afterward is limited only by your imagination and flexibility. Either way, buying essentials and splitting or recuperating the cost can be miles cheaper than renting if you shop smart and follow through.

RULE #19: Don't ever buy new what you can source used!

P.S.: Don't forget to use your powers of ninja negotiation to work down the cost and get a bulk discount whenever possible!

Here's a brief list of shareables to get your gears turning, but challenge yourself to find other ways to reduce, reuse, and save green while being green!

- Dresses
- Lanterns/lighting
- Votive holders and candles
- Manzanita branches (for centerpieces, ceremony decor, or your guest book/wishing tree)
- Tulle and ribbon
- Bathroom baskets and accessories
- Crafting tools, supplies, and machines
- Jewelry, shawls, and purses
- Buffet vessels
- Linens
- Sign holders
- Frames
- Centerpiece parts
- Vases
- Flower girl basket/ring pillow
- Mason jars/other glassware
- Dishware
- Paper for invitations (this is where bulk discounts come in handy)
- Crafted bouquets
- Crafted centerpieces
- Terrariums
- Utility items (extension cords, fishing line, hooks, duct tape)

re-up: one couple's trash can be your treasure

Even if it's not in the cards for you to find a Bride$hare buddy before your wedding, there are other ways to score hot deals on eco-friendly items to keep the karma rolling, as well as make some money back *after* the wedding.

Using Craigslist, eBay, classified sections of wedding websites, or some of the great new sites specifically geared toward bridal resale (such as Tradesy, Encore Bridal, Once Wed, PreOwnedWed dingDresses.com), couples often sell off all kinds of recyclables from their weddings, from designer dresses and decor to leftover DIY project items. You can score mind-blowing deals on new or gently used unique pieces. I even found photographers offering free engagement sessions to build their portfolios in wedding website classifieds, which is also a great opportunity to test-run a young, and likely affordable, photographer's style and personality for your wedding! Don't forget to pay it forward by re-listing your stuff after you say "I do," and recoup some costs for yourself like a boss!

Buying handmade and/or local products are some of my other favorite methods of sustainable shopping. Sites with independent artists like Etsy, Wedzu, and ArtFire are a veritable treasure trove of handmade goodness that sings with style. From dresses to jewelry, decor and more, you can support indie artists and feel the love oozing from their glue guns straight to your heart. Local flea markets and craft fairs can net you some unique goodies, rich with character and often inexpensive, allowing you to express yourselves and your style with budget-savvy flair.

fashionably green

A brand-new, bleached-white wedding gown that you only wear for one day? One that may even have been constructed overseas and shipped to you? Not to be a Debbie Downer here, ladies, but the gown is a great place to go green! You've got plenty of options:

- Shop consignment or bridal resale stores and websites. Brick-and-mortar locations for these shops are cropping up more and more frequently, owing to demand, but you can find almost any gown style online via sites like Tradesy, Encore Bridal, PreOwnedWeddingDressses.com, and even eBay or Craigslist!

    HINT: Find the gown in a retail store and try it on before ordering online, to make sure you know your size. Don't be afraid to message the seller inquiring about quality and damage before you commit.

- Rent! It's a great way to get a gorgeous gown at a fraction of the price. RentTheRunway.com is a good start, or Google "wedding dress rental" for local options.

- Is there a gown in your family that would suit your style? Or enough fabric from a gown or two that you can have redesigned from the dresses of those who came before you? Repurposing family gowns carries special significance, and hiring a seamstress to build a "new" gown from existing fabric can save you a bundle compared with buying a new one. I once heard about a bride who wore a patchwork gown made from scraps of fabric from every woman in her family. I freaking love that idea!

- Eco-friendly fabrics have come a long way in recent years, and designers are embracing them more than ever. From vintage fabrics to unbleached cotton or muslin, these dresses look no less beautiful or newer than bleached, polyester, and tulle gowns.
- A local designer, Deborah Lindquist, used a combination of vintage lace and organic, unbleached muslin (eco-friendlier than fabrics that involve pesticides, chemicals, and genetic engineering) to create my stunning couture gown; and it was one of the loveliest creations I've ever laid eyes on. She also uses repurposed cashmere for many of her designs—a perfect fabric for a bridal shrug or winter bridal gown.

Keep an open mind when you shop around; you just never know what you might find! But if you must buy new, consider reselling it after your own wedding, and letting your dress go on to make another bride just as happy as you were.

SOMETHING OLD, MADE NEW! A VINTAGE DISHWARE REGISTRY

We got the idea to register for vintage dishware after seeing the plates of our dreams on the set of a television sitcom taping that we attended. I was flat-out drooling for their bright yellow and orange poppy print, and even Hunter gave them a "Hells, yeah, that's cool." We scampered over after the taping to check the stamp on the plates, ran home to Google it, and mentally filed it away. After a long and fruitless search for something new (and more readily available) that we loved just as much for our registry, we finally decided to go our own way and say "We do" to the first dishes to steal our poppy-lovin' hearts. It was the perfect decision for us. In fact, we ended up buying vintage silverware on eBay to go along with it. Keep on reading to find out how you can integrate auction pieces into your registry.

The benefits of vintage dishware are threefold:

1. It's usually more budget-friendly. The set we picked out cost less than most sets we saw at Crate & Barrel or Macy's.

2. It's more eco-friendly. Reuse is a better choice than buying new, any day!

3. It's often more finger-friendly. My clumsy self excels at breaking dishes. Vintage dishware can be sturdier and more break-resistant, keeping your wedding dishes safer for years to come!

Search at sites like Metlox California; Replacements, Ltd.; Etsy; and eBay. You can also try flea markets and antique bazaars in your town, like the Pasadena Rose Bowl Flea Market in Southern California. And who says your set needs to be matchy-matchy? Pick out an eclectic mix of dishes that speaks to you, and create your own rules!

There are also some progressively fierce companies taking vintage dishware/china and turning it into something modern, like Esther Derkx, who screen-prints modern figures onto vintage plates for a delectable fresh impression!

"But, Dana!" you protest. "How do I register for something so random? Won't it be challenging for my guests to find/pay for?" Woman, get thee online! Tons of new alternative or cash gift registry sites abound, where you can register for items you find anywhere, in brick-and-mortar stores or on the Internet. Check out sites like Honeyfund .com, SimpleRegistry, Deposit a Gift, Honeymoon Pixie, and Zankyou, among others.

Your guests can donate funds toward the purchase of any items that cannot be purchased online. It's a convenient way to unleash yourselves from single-store registries. After we completed the purchase of our flatware in an online auction, we manually listed the item and price on our online registry site, and a friend "reimbursed" the gift to us via PayPal. (Thanks again, Jason!) Or, you can contact a vintage dishware-replacement company and ask if they'll set up a registry for you. Many offer that service these days. And remember our mantra? It never hurts to ask!

These sites are also a great solution for the more expensive items that are apt to end up on your registry, whether they be a high-end cookware set or a couch you've lusted for. Every dollar your guests put into the registry comes to you in the form of cash, usually with a nominal percentage withdrawn by the host registry. It's also a super-handy way to register for your honeymoon! Who wouldn't want to buy a newly minted married couple some mutual massages on the beach?

five ways to rock your cash registry

1 Get what you want from whence you want it. If it's not available online, you can snap a photo and upload it with a description and price so people can fund your purchase of said coveted item—even if it's from that creepy flea market–style shop down the street that your friends don't understand why you like.

2 As discussed, registering for recycled or pre-owned items and antiques is great for the earth, and your style.

3 Bank big-ticket items. An expensive knife, cookware sets, furniture pieces, or decor items might be too big a gift to ask any one person to buy, but cash registries allow a gaggle of guests to contribute partial funding to items of their choosing—perfect for a family to go in on together and treat you to something that would also be hard to splurge on yourself.

4 Sweeten up your honeymoon. Everything from your flight costs to romantic excursions can be listed, and therefore, gifted. Let your guests give you the gift of experience, and be sure to send them postcards from wherever you wander, thanking them for the great memories!

5 Feather your nest egg. The best part about cash registries is that, at the end of the day, you can withdraw your dough and use it however you wish! If you change your mind about something you've listed, or decide that sticking that scratch in a high-yield savings account would be a better investment in your future . . . the money is yours to do with what you will! And nobody will ever be the wiser.

11

The rehearsal

The rehearsal dinner

The day of

When the party's over

The Big Day

Congratulations! You've made it to your wedding day, with your sanity (mostly) intact, and your budget (we hope) in check. Today, you arrive at the altar single; you'll voice your vows and marry your best friend. Your lips will meet, and *justlikethat,* you'll be married. A newlywed. And a whole new chapter of life will begin! I am so happy for you!

There are still a few murky waters to navigate before the night ends, however, and I have some handy tips to help you survive, enjoy yourselves as much as possible, and enhance the experience in a handful of surprising ways. The best part? Most of my tips cost zero dollars, but their effects can be truly priceless.

First, let's rewind to the day before, shall we?

the rehearsal

Usually the day before your wedding, the rehearsal is a simple walk-through of the ceremony and surrounding logistics. It's a chance to work out the timing, review the order of the processional and recessional, and get a sense of what it feels like to stand at the altar, looking into the eyes of your future spouse. You won't be saying your actual vows, just plotting through the various segments of the ceremony and practicing the "moving from here to there" of it all.

The only people necessary to have present for the rehearsal are you and your partner, your officiant, the wedding party, parents on both sides, and your planner or coordinator. If you have special guests performing or doing a reading, you might want them there as well. Anyone else is completely optional.

the rehearsal dinner

If your wedding day is the big game, your rehearsal dinner is the tailgating party. You'll have a chance to spend time with the people closest to you, to celebrate your wedding party and parents, and to thank them for their support. I love the fact that your wedding party and families on both sides can cut loose and get to know one another better before the big day. The rehearsal dinner is traditionally hosted by the groom's family, but those hard-and-fast rules about who pays for what have long since blurred into a gray area.

The dinner can be anything from a casual pizza party at home to a fancy dinner in a private room at a restaurant. It's really up to you and your budget, and all the ideas from Chapter 2 regarding engagement parties apply to the rehearsal dinner as well. One of the most memorable rehearsal dinners I've attended was a casual picnic at the beach, catered by the family of the bride.

> HINT: If your wedding venue caters internally, you might be able to negotiate a good deal on rehearsal dinner service through them as an add-on to your contract.

In terms of whom you include for the rehearsal dinner, etiquette generally suggests that it's the same people as present at your rehearsal, plus any friends or family who have traveled from out of the area to attend your wedding. The concept is that they're probably shacking up at a hotel or a friend's house to be there for you, so it's a thoughtful gesture for you to offer them a decent meal.

Again, whether you invite out-of-towners all depends on your comfort level and budget, but if you aren't going to include them in the rehearsal dinner, consider giving them a heads-up ahead of time because an expectation might already be in place. A simple denotation on the wedding website or itinerary would suffice, such as "Rehearsal dinner for immediate family and bridal party."

The rehearsal dinner is the time to give thank-you gifts to your bridal party and your parents. Some couples choose to do this discreetly, and some like to make each gift into a toast to the recipient. After your rehearsal dinner, whether or not you plan to spend the night with

your partner or sleep in separate beds, I highly recommend taking a few last moments together as single people, and practice your first dance. It doesn't matter if you've planned choreography or a simple prom sway, taking the time together, then—feeling each other's bodies and hearing the music and enjoying that calm before tomorrow's storm—will help center you and bring you back to the point: tomorrow is about marriage. Not the wedding, but marriage.

When you set your alarm for the next day, give yourself an extra hour or half hour, if you can. Better to have too much time to get ready than be rushing out the door to the aisle. You never know what might come up!

> HOT TIP: If nervous jitters are keeping you awake, and you have eight hours before you must be up, take a Benadryl or melatonin to help you float away to sleep (with your doctor's permission, of course)!

the day of

WHEN YOU WAKE UP

Take your time alone in bed for a bit. Think about your vows, maybe even write your partner a letter from the perspective of that morning, which you can choose to have delivered to your beloved before the ceremony, gift to him/her later that evening, or even save for your first anniversary together. If you'd prefer to keep those feelings private, perhaps journal for yourself any feelings and/or fears you might have. Getting it out of your head and onto paper will help you quiet your mental chatter so that you're ready to receive everything that comes at you.

One of the greatest gifts on the morning of my wedding was the relief that came with waking up and realizing: there's no going back. All the little details we cut away because of time or budget constraints, all the things we might've overlooked or forgotten, anything that could go wrong throughout the day—none of it really mattered because, at that point, there was nothing more I could do to control it. And I just let it go. That was one of the best feelings of the day, actually, since it allowed me to be present for the rest of it, rather than judging it from the outside.

 **RULE #13:** Forget your troubles, c'mon get happy.

Take a moment on the morning of to recognize your fears and worries, and then consciously hand them over to the Universe, your God, fate . . . whatever "higher power" allows you to release control and trust that at this point, what will be, will be. My personal favorite way to release worry is the Serenity Prayer (more commonly known as the twelve-step prayer). The phrasing of it is just right for recognizing that it's okay to be afraid, but there's only so much you can do. The rest will unfold with or without your worry.

If you have any wiggle room in your budget, a massage can be a great way to unwind and take some quiet time for yourself. My sister Kim does bodywork, as I mentioned earlier, and having her spending that time with me, helping me relax, was absolutely priceless. I felt that I stood taller and was more grounded at the altar, thanks to her magic hands. If that's not possible, a long, hot shower can do the trick as well. Treat yourself to a nice body scrub, take your time shaving your legs and moisturizing, and breathe deeply and evenly as you go along. (Don't forget the shower cap if your stylist instructed you not to wash on the day of!)

EARLY IN THE DAY

- **Eat.** Make sure you eat, even just a small meal, in the hours before your wedding. You can't predict when you'll get your next chance before dinner, and all that excitement can leave a girl feeling quite peckish and woozy. No one needs the bride fainting at the altar! A healthy salad with protein is a great option, but treat yourself to whatever sounds good!

- **Hydrate.** I cannot stress this enough. You must try to always have a glass of water in hand, or nearby, up to an hour before your ceremony. Staying well hydrated improves every single bodily function, especially in helping you regulate your body temperature, think clearly, and hold your Champagne better. It also helps your skin glow and keeps your lips moist, so it does health and beauty double-duty! But, yes, please do stop a good hour before you go, to avoid last minute nerve-induced pee-jitters at the altar. You're welcome, in advance, for that.

- **Skip the cell.** Early in the day, hand off your phone to your maid of honor, mother, sister, coordinator, or someone else responsible and trustworthy, so that person can handle last-minute "when, where, and who" calls, allowing you to focus just on the day without constant interruption.

A WHILE BEFORE THE CEREMONY

If you and your partner have decided to shoot your wedding photos ahead of time to get you to the cocktail hour sooner, make sure you plan something special so that you're photographed during your "first look"—that moment when you first see each other in your full wedding regalia.

I also recommend that about 30 minutes before the ceremony, you take a break and part to separate areas of the venue. Rebuilding a bit of that anticipation will help your walk down the aisle have more magic than if you were just hanging out five minutes previously. Of course, if you've decided to stay separated beforehand, just skip this step!

JUST BEFORE THE CEREMONY

- **Skip to the loo.** It may take some finagling in your big fluffy dress, but a last-minute trip to the potty will keep you from that "gotta pee" distraction during your ceremony. I found this moment so hilarious that I actually had it photo-documented on my big day! Settle down, now: it was adorable, and modest enough to be Facebook-worthy, I promise.

  HINT: Squat down facing the toilet tank rather than sitting away from it. That's right, I'm telling you to use the toilet backward. It's easier to gather and hold the front of your dress and let the back drape over the outside of the bowl to ensure an ... um ... unobstructed flow.

- **Rinse and spit.** A quick swish of Listerine will ensure that your first kiss won't suffer from the crazy dry-mouth funk that nerves can sometimes induce just before your big moment. The minty freshness can also inject a bright how's-your-father into your brain and help reinvigorate you.

- **Tighten up.** If you're going strapless, a great cheat is to do 10 to 20 wall push-ups right before you walk the aisle. It'll enhance your muscle definition and get your blood flowing to pump up your natural rosy glow. A lineup of brides and 'maids doing push-ups in their gowns also makes for a fun, irreverent pre-wedding photo.

- **Take a moment.** Twice. Spend a couple of minutes with whomever will be escorting you down the aisle, just before you go, and tell your escort how much his or her support means to you. If it's your father, there's nothing quite like that first moment he sees you all done up. Relish it.

    Then, at the top of the aisle, just when you appear before the crowd, stop for a second. Look at that space, at all the people who've come to support your union. Look at that altar, lined with your nearest and dearest, and helmed by your partner. Take a deep breath, and enjoy that walk to meet him or her there. The best advice I was given before my wedding, I will now pass on to you because I found it so effective and special:

RULE #14: Take it all in!

Then find your partner's eyes and focus only on him as you make your way down. You'll stay in the moment and share an intimacy and anticipation that can never be replaced. I swear, I felt as though I were floating toward Hunter as his gaze drew me there. Everything else faded away. It was just him and me, discovering each other anew again after so many years.

AFTER THE CEREMONY

Find a quiet corner or room to disappear into for 10 or so minutes just after the ceremony, and spend that time with your new spouse. These are your first moments as newlyweds; enjoy them. Your photographer can get some shots without you in this time. P.S. This is a good time to make out like crazy.

AT THE RECEPTION

- **Keep hydrating.** Try to balance every boozy beverage against a glass of water to stay in the clear and prevent sloppy bride syndrome.
- **Eat.** It's sometimes the hardest thing to do at your own wedding, annoyingly, especially if you're planning to greet your guests at their tables during dinner rather than in a receiving line after the ceremony. But don't let it sway you. If you must, shove it all down right away when everyone is seated, but even if you eat your whole meal in 5 minutes, do eat your whole meal. You've paid enough for it—you ought to enjoy it!
  - **Smooch your spouse.** A lot. (Notice how I said "spouse"? Yeah, baby.)
  - **Relax.** This is your party, and you've already accomplished the biggest goal of the day: you're married! So if you haven't yet, now is the time to really let go, kick back, and enjoy every moment of the celebration. You've earned it!

when the party's over

Graciously thank everyone for coming, and retire to your honeymoon suite. Now, this might seem a bit off-color, but, hey, it's me we're dealing with here! So now, I'll give to you some of the best advice Hunter received before the wedding. You can pass it along to your own partner as either a modest hint or an enthusiastic demand. No matter what happens, "nail her in the dress." Fancy wedding lingerie be damned, I say! Save it for the next morning. Just hike up your skirt, and give that bed the newlywed treatment, proper!

Now, as you float off to sleep, say good night to your new spouse, calling each other by your new married names: "Sweet dreams, wife." Or "Nighty-night, husband."

Epilogue
THE SMALL STUFF
REALLY IS SMALL STUFF

At the end of the day, I hope your wedding is as magical and wondrous as my own was. I still regard it as one of the happiest and most beautiful days of my life.

But not everything went right. And this is important.

We were behind on the to-do list. The morning of my wedding, I spent an hour on the laptop designing our programs, and I sent my dad scrambling to the print shop to get them ready for the ceremony.

Our second shooter was two hours late to meet the groom's party for "getting ready" photos and ran out of film 10 minutes into the ceremony. Which means that we also had no photos whatsoever of the cocktail hour because our lead photographer was with us doing portraits.

I had lost so much weight in the weeks before the wedding that my dress ended up being 2 inches too long, which resulted in me putting my heel through the back of my gown when we stomped the glass. When we arrived at the reception, my dress designer, who was (luckily for me) in attendance, joined me in a bathroom and cut 2 inches off the bottom hem.

The shuttle bus got ticketed while waiting for the men at their hotel, adding an unbudgeted $80 to our bill.

I totally forgot my bouquet for the walk down the aisle (because I was using my free hand to hold up the front of my dress so I wouldn't trip on it!), but it was sneaked up to the altar by my coordinator so I could hold it briefly while there.

We completely missed the cocktail hour while shooting family and bridal portraits after the ceremony.

I got only one shot in our photo booth at the reception because I wasn't aware they were packing up shop.

I sprained my ankle, badly, one hour before the end of the night, thanks to a combination of mojito drinking and "getting too low" on a pole while dancing to my amazing DJ's jams. I was carried off the dance floor. My (amazing) matron-of-honor sister came up and said (in her best faux sympathetic voice): "Aw, did you huwt youwr ankooo?" Then, "Well, get up and keep dancing. It's your freaking wedding!" And I did. Oh, yes, I did. The next morning, my ankle was the size of a soccer ball, and I spent our honeymoon either in a wheelchair or on crutches, and I couldn't walk on it for a month afterward. (Totally worth it, btw.) All I have to say is, thank goodness we didn't book an adventure-heavy honeymoon and instead spent most of the time on the beach!

There were other little mishaps, too, but none of them fazed us much. We were so in the moment, caught up in the joy of the day, that we couldn't even sweat the small stuff. In fact, looking back, I love those moments the most. Because we're humans, and life is messy and imperfect. So it follows that a wedding should be, too (to some extent). Unless you're deliberately looking for things to go wrong, chances are you'll barely notice if they do.

So, if I can impart to you any wisdom at all as you close this book and move forward with your wedding and your marriage, let it be this:

RULE #15: No matter what happens, remember that the focus of your wedding day is to make your vows and start your marriage.

It's not to wear the dress. Not to eat the food. Not to dance the dances, or open the gifts, or throw the bouquet, look perfect in photos, or have everything match. So don't worry that people will think you're "cheap" if you DIY your own flowers, omit the favors, iPod your dance floor, or whatever the corners you cut may be.

Don't fret about what they'll think, whether you want to be married by a pastor or a pagan queen. It's your day. Do it your way. Your guests are there to celebrate you and your love, not to criticize your chair selection. And if they do, that's their problem, not yours.

No. It is to marry the person you love and begin a new phase of commitment that will be just as, if not more, challenging than most things in your life up until this point.

My best advice? Just have FUN. The rest, and we hope, the *best*, is yet to come.

appendixes

A **Sample Budgets from Real Brides**
- UNDER $5K
- UNDER $10K
- UNDER $15K
- UNDER $20K
- UNDER $25K
- UNDER $30K
- OVER $30K

B **Recipes for Happy Bellies and Full Wallets**
- BEVERAGES FOR GROWN-UPS
- RECIPES THAT ROCK
- HOW TO FEED 40 PEOPLE FOR $3 EACH

C **Glossary of Wedding Terms and Acronyms**

D **Resources**

Sample Budgets

FROM REAL BRIDES

Attention voyeurs among you! Hear ye! Hear ye! This section is for you! Because not every couple divvies up their funds exactly the same way (nor should they!), we reached out to the masses and pulled together a wide variety of budgets with detailed breakdowns just for you!

Studying how other couples allocate their money can be really eye-opening in terms of helping you to understand how to set your own priorities and direct your dollars thusly. Also, feel free to let it alleviate any guilt that might come from the feeling that you're "splurging" on any one or two things. Everybody does! It's part of the joy of spending what feels to be an obscene amount of money on a single event. Relish the ability to buy what matters to you.

When you look over these budgets, compare them side by side. Notice what couples splurged on or what they chose to omit, and how much that can vary based on people's priorities.

Under $5K

················· Meg and Mathew ·················

LOCATION: DeFuniak Springs, Florida

GUEST COUNT: 50

VENUE: Free
(their church)

FOOD/DRINK: $600
(reception food prepared by some amazing church ladies: heavy appetizers, sweet tea, two cases of Champagne, and a keg of Bud Light)

ATTIRE/ACCESSORIES: $1,028
(Mori Lee wedding dress from Dazzling Prom and Bridal; groom's suit from Men's Wearhouse)

FLOWERS: $350
(four bridesmaid bouquets and two large bouquets for the altar from McLean's Florist & Gifts, plus a DIY brooch bouquet made with antique brooches that belonged to the bride's grandmother)

DECOR: $100
(Mason jars filled with M&M's, card box from Oriental Trading, serving set, guest book/pen and fall leaves from Hobby Lobby. The couple borrowed cowboy hats and boots from friends and family to fill in centerpieces.)

DJ/BAND/ENTERTAINMENT: $500
(DJ at reception, $300; bagpiper during ceremony, $200)

PHOTOGRAPHY: $300
for ceremony and formal portraits (Simply Gorgeous Photography by Brenda)

VIDEOGRAPHY: N/A

CAKE: $100
(made by a lady from church)

FAVORS: $50
(beer koozies and cookie cutter card favors from Oriental Trading)

INVITATIONS/PRINTING/ POSTAGE: $95
(Smith's Signs & Printing: magnet save-the-dates, cardstock invites, and address labels)

HAIR/MAKEUP: Free
(done by bride's sister)

WEDDING PARTY: $92
(bridesmaid and groomsmen gifts)

WEDDING BANDS: $50
(thanks to a pretty sweet gift certificate!)

COORDINATOR/PLANNER: N/A

OFFICIANT: Free
(couple's priest)

LICENSE: $93

OTHER: N/A

TOTAL: $3,358

LOCATION: Depauw, Indiana

GUEST COUNT: 100

VENUE: $727
(Cardinal House Lodge)
"We wanted to do a camp theme but also have an indoor option in case the weather was bad. My mom found this place by chance and it was perfect. We told the lodge owner we were having a family reunion of sorts. This fib was to avoid any extra charges they may have added because it was a wedding."

FOOD/DRINK: $750
(smart budget alert! The bride and groom's families industriously prepared all of the food themselves.)

ATTIRE/ACCESSORIES: $268
(Dorothy Perkins dress, $56; bride and groom's shoes plus groom's attire, $212 from Off Broadway Shoes and Express)
"I wanted a nonformal, nontraditional dress that I could wear again. Nick also wanted something that he could use again, so we opted to buy clothes off the rack from places where we would normally shop."

FLOWERS: $50
(Kroger)
"I am very indecisive, so I knew that if I ordered flowers in advance that I might not want them by the time the big day rolled around. We checked out some other flower shops around town a few days before and they didn't have the selection that the Kroger Floral Department had. I bought bunches of various flowers and the bridal party made their own bouquets at lunch before the ceremony. Everyone got to personalize them."

DECOR: $317
(muslin and burlap from Fabric Direct; ribbon, canvas, ink, markers, etc., from Hobby Lobby; table candles from IKEA)
"This was a great idea, because now I have lots of materials left over to do crafting at home! This amount includes supplies for the homemade gifts I gave our wedding party, too!"

DJ/BAND/ENTERTAINMENT: $64
(sound system rental from Doo Wop Shop)
"Pretty much everyone has an iPod or some type of device that can play music so we thought the wedding guests could be our DJs. I was actually surprised at how inexpensive this sound system rental was for the weekend. It included a microphone and auxiliary cable so anyone could plug in their device and play a song at our party."

PHOTOGRAPHY: Free
"We really lucked out in having some great amateur photographers in our wedding party and as guests. Befriend photographers!"

(continues)

VIDEOGRAPHY: N/A

CAKE: $125

(made by the bride's aunt)
"Growing up I always looked forward to spending the holidays at my aunt's house because she makes the most delicious candies and sweets. Having her make the cake and cupcakes was the obvious choice in keeping with the DIY family-oriented theme."

FAVORS: $15

(succulents came from bride's garden, terra-cotta pots were upcycled!)
"My parents have a micro-farm and keep a lot of planting materials on hand. We repotted some overgrown hens and chicks succulents and aloe plants into the upcycled pots and used them as centerpieces and wedding favors. All we ended up paying for was potting soil. This was one of my favorite ideas. (If you are planning on doing this, make sure you do it at least two months in advance to give the plants a chance to re-root, and discard any that don't make it through the transplant.)"

INVITATIONS/PRINTING/ POSTAGE: Free

(gifted through the bride's work)
"We totally lucked out on this. Just sayin'."

HAIR/MAKEUP: Free
"I don't really wear too much make-up and I feel uncomfortable when I do, so I opted to do it myself instead of having a stranger pile the stuff on my face. My friend Wendy also cut my hair the day before for free as a wedding gift. Befriend hairstylists!"

WEDDING PARTY: See Decor

WEDDING BANDS: $500

(Kay Jewelers)
"My engagement ring is an heirloom Art Deco ring that first belonged to Nick's great grandmother. For the wedding bands I wanted something simple, so I just got a small white gold band that complements my engagement ring. We went to Kay Jewelers when they were having a sale."

COORDINATOR/PLANNER: N/A

OFFICIANT: Free
(groom's sister)

LICENSE: $35

OTHER: $674
($534 tent rental [Rent a Tent]; $140 portable toilets)
"This was not in the original budget plan, but since there was a chance of rain my mom ordered a tent the week before, and the portable toilets since the lodge was older, and the owners were worried about the septic system not being able to handle our number of guests."

TOTAL: $3,525

LOCATION: Palos Verdes, California

GUEST COUNT: 80

VENUE: $800
(Point Vicente Interpretive Center)

FOOD/DRINK: About $900
(catered by Open Sesame Mediterranean Grill in Long Beach)
"We served Lebanese food, buffet style in foil trays on paper plates. DELICIOUS! My guests fell on it like locusts. We spent about $100 on soft drinks. I know we cheaped out here by not having booze, but we had an early wedding in a remote location and our justification was that we didn't want to have any guests hit the road drunk."

ATTIRE/ACCESSORIES: $200
"I wore a black dress from Nordstrom, $100, and red shoes from Nordstrom, $100. He wore clothes he already had."

FLOWERS: $150
"Todd went to L.A. Flower Mart early on the day of the wedding and spent about $150 on Gerbera daisies for the tables and peonies to make my bouquet out of. Sure, it was stressful getting/arranging flowers on the day of, and I should have had a trusted friend do it. However, they were fresh and gorgeous and CHEAP!"

DECOR: $250
"We had white Christmas tree lights strung up everywhere. Table centerpieces were made out of white rectangular Japanese plates (that we use for dinner now!), vases made from tall Libbey glasses that we ordered in bulk from Surfas Commercial Kitchen Supply, and Japanese lanterns made by hot-gluing Japanese paper around other glasses that we bought in bulk."

DJ/BAND/ENTERTAINMENT: Free
"We plugged an iPod into the venue's sound system."

PHOTOGRAPHY: $500
(their friend Tracy did double-duty as a friendor)

VIDEOGRAPHY: N/A
"I really didn't want to have to worry about if I looked good on camera all day long."

CAKE: $100
"My stepmother got a chocolate cake from a Japanese bakery."

FAVORS: N/A
(omitted)

INVITATIONS/PRINTING/ POSTAGE: $230
(Wedding Paper Divas)

HAIR/MAKEUP: Free
"My friends gave me a gift certificate to a salon at my bridal shower, and another friend did my makeup for me."

(continues)

WEDDING PARTY: N/A

"We didn't have any wedding attendants."

WEDDING BANDS: $300

"I bought his ring for $300. I only ever wanted one ring, so we used my engagement ring from Tracy Allen in Los Angeles."

COORDINATOR/PLANNER: $200

"The wedding was largely planned and coordinated by myself and the groom, plus two girls that I work with (we produce a film festival together so they know how to put on an event). I paid them each $100, and they ran the event at the venue, set up/cleaned up, worked with the food delivery guy, etc."

OFFICIANT: Free

(their friend officiated)

LICENSE: $120

OTHER: N/A

"So, we were aiming for $3,000, but went a little bit over. It was a FUN wedding. Totally informal and DIY, but with great people and great food. My biggest piece of advice is that it's better to get really cheap but totally delicious food than to get served catered food. Nobody remembers the chicken breast they had at that one wedding, but everyone remembers our awesome food."

TOTAL: $3,850

Under $10K

LOCATION: Pasadena, California

GUEST COUNT: 68

VENUE: $385

"Our ceremony was at the South Pasadena Public Library, and our reception was at a restaurant in Old Town Pasadena called POP Champagne and Dessert Bar. The library requires a three-hour minimum rental block for the community room (the oldest part of the library, built in 1907 and beautiful), and $60/hour was far and away the cheapest option we found—not to mention the prettiest! We got three hours for a rehearsal and three hours for the day of, and also rented their sound system for $25. Total cost, $385."

FOOD/DRINK: $3,800

including taxes and tip

"We had an open bar (beer/wine and Champagne cocktails), three passed appetizers, three entrée items (sliders, chicken, and truffle mac and cheese), and three desserts chosen from the restaurant's menu. POP was completely flexible with us on budget, and allowed us to dictate how many people would be using the open bar (as in, we did not pay for that for all of our guests— only the ones we knew would be drinking).

"Keeping in mind that it was at a restaurant, this was our total cost—no renting tables and chairs, no catering to deal with, no major decorating to do, no centerpieces to worry about—everything was taken care of! Not only was it smart financially, but it also made the planning process SO much easier! It ended up being so affordable, we invited twenty more guests than we originally planned for."

ATTIRE/ACCESSORIES: $745

"After trying it on, I knew I wanted to wear the Avila Bay dress from Dolly Couture. However, even at the (relatively affordable) $800 mark, it was a bit pricey for me. A couple of months later, I found someone on an online forum selling it, never worn, for $250! It was a bit big, but even after spending $150 for alterations, it came in at $400. I found my shoes on Amazon for $80, my headband at Anthropologie ($32), and my faux fur jacket at, of all places, Forever 21 for $25.

"We also went ahead and bought new clothes for the groom. He works at Banana Republic, so we took advantage of his employee discount to buy new slacks for $35. He wore a white dress shirt and gray blazer he already owned, over a vest we found at Urban Outfitters for $75, and a $13 tie from H&M. His shoes, from DSW, wound up being the most expensive item at $85. The nice thing: he'll wear them again!"

(continues)

FLOWERS: $50

"I made bouquets for myself and my MOH from flowers I got at Trader Joe's for $25. The groom used succulents and some small flowers for the boutonnieres, which with supplies, also cost about $25. We decided against using flowers in any of the decor, partly because I am allergic to most cut flowers, but also to save more money."

DECOR: $75

"We did some serious DIY for our wedding, not necessarily to save money but because we are both pretty handy people and enjoy working on projects together. All of our supplies cost roughly $75, and we still have a lot of stuff left over. I also plan on reselling them to another couple afterward, to recoup the cost."

DJ/BAND/ENTERTAINMENT: Free

"We kept the music the restaurant normally uses, since we didn't want to dance and it just wasn't so important to us to have a band. It fell into the category of something that would be nice if we had the money, but at the end of the day was not critical to us having an awesome day. We made our own playlist for before the ceremony and for our processional and recessional, that was played through the library sound system."

PHOTOGRAPHY: Free

"This is where we got really lucky. My dad's best friend's son is a photographer, and agreed to do our wedding pictures for free, in trade for my dad's help on a few projects (since he is also a photographer)."

VIDEOGRAPHY: N/A

"We recorded the ceremony with a video camera, but again, videography of the whole day was just not important to us. At any rate, we have enough friends with smartphones to capture any moments the photographer missed."

CAKE: $50

"We used the vendor the restaurant normally works with for cakes (Violet's Cakes). Since we were already providing dessert, we got a 6-inch cake just to cut."

FAVORS: $50

"We made cider/wine mulling spices for everyone! Total cost for bags, labels, and spices was $50."

INVITATIONS/PRINTING/ POSTAGE: $150

"We didn't do save-the-dates (since all of the guests were close friends or family and already knew the date). We bought our invites through A Printable Press ($79), printed them at home on 5x7 cards from Paper Source, and did an e-mail RSVP to save on postage."

HAIR/MAKEUP: $100

"I went to Sephora for a makeup consultation, which is free with a $50 purchase. So I got some new makeup ($100), and did it myself. I rarely wear makeup anyway, so I was more comfortable being in total control of how I looked. I also did my own hair (it's short and doesn't require much work anyway)."

WEDDING PARTY: $30

"We only had a maid of honor and best man, so this was essentially free. My MOH bought her own dress (we intentionally planned to make it affordable for her, and to make it something she would wear again). We bought our best man a tie and slacks using Kyle's Banana Republic discount, which came to about $30."

WEDDING BANDS: $110

"There was a mix-up with my engagement ring, and to make up for it they gave us my wedding band for free! Both were from Turtle Love Co., and the total cost was $1,800. (This we had saved for separately, so I don't really consider it part of our wedding budget.) The groom's band was custom made by a seller on Etsy, and cost $110 with shipping from England."

COORDINATOR/PLANNER: N/A

"We did everything ourselves, without a planner (although I did seriously consider hiring one at a few points). I did hire someone from TaskRabbit for $25 to clean up the ceremony space after we were finished."

OFFICIANT: Free

"Done by our good friend Ben and his wife, Kirsten."

LICENSE: $115

(including a mailed copy of the certificate)

OTHER: $25

(ceremony cleanup)

TOTAL: $5,685

···················· **Dana and Sheldon** ····················

LOCATION: Indianola, Oklahoma

GUEST COUNT: 150

VENUE: Free

(bride's family ranch)
"We chose to have the wedding at my parents' ranch because it would be a more relaxed environment. We didn't like the rules or the prices that were involved with renting venues and wanted our guests to be able to stay as late as they liked without having to worry about cleaning up everything immediately.

It made everyone's stress a lot lower and made us feel like we could truly enjoy the day."

FOOD/DRINK: $1,500

(entire meal and cupcakes were prepared by bride's family, including home-smoked meat. They even had a barbecue sauce fountain—how great is that?)
"Since many guests were traveling more than two hours for the wedding we wanted to feed them a great meal before they had to leave to drive back home. There

(continues)

weren't any options for catering in Indianola and my dad's barbecue is awesome, so we decided to have him smoke brisket and chicken and family members made sides for us."

ATTIRE/ACCESSORIES: $1,800
(includes DIY bridal gown, bridesmaids' dresses sewn by the bride and her mother, ring bearer and flower girls' outfits from Ross, and all the men's ties were ordered from a seller on Etsy)
"We spent a lot here because I wanted dupioni silk for my dress and we decided to buy as much of the wedding party's clothing as we could. We pretty much paid for everything but the guys' suits."

FLOWERS: $250
(Sam's Club, arranged by a family friend)
"I wanted really simple, not overly arranged, flowers. Sam's had daisies that we could buy in bulk. These flowers were awesome! I can't recommend them enough. They came two days before the wedding, we soaked them in water, and they were beautiful the next day. Since daisies are fairly hardy, they were still going strong a week after the wedding and my mom used the flowers for a church dinner the next weekend."

DECOR: $650
(includes favors, all DIY)
"I made everything; all of our stationery (save-the-dates, invitations, thank-you cards), the centerpieces, buntings, cupcake toppers, boutonnieres, guest book love notes, our photo booth, button

wedding favors and packaging, an activity table, handmade coloring books for the kids, and the napkins. My dad and the men in our family built our dance floor, cut logs for aisle runners, made rustic wedding signs to have in a few places on the highway to lead to the wedding, and turned my parents' ranch into a beautiful place for a wedding."

DJ/BAND/ENTERTAINMENT: $70
"We rented a sound system (lumped into the party rental price) and made playlists for our iPod, including all our favorite songs. At the end of the night our friends were able to plug in their phones and play whatever music they wanted to hear."

PHOTOGRAPHY: $800
"I wanted a well-known (read expensive) photographer whose work I had followed for some time. Sheldon didn't want a professional photographer at all. We compromised for a more inexpensive photographer that I thought was great. Her work has continued to get better since our wedding and I'm so glad we hired her because I love our photos!"

VIDEOGRAPHY: N/A

CAKE: See Food/Drink
"My mom has decorated cakes for a long time and I have a love of cupcakes so we decided to have family members make four dozen cupcakes in a certain flavor and we decorated all of them the day before the wedding. It was fun getting to spend this decorating time with my mom, aunts, and cousins bonding over icing."

FAVORS: See Decor

INVITATIONS/PRINTING/ POSTAGE: $400 (DIY)

"We saved money by designing and printing most of our paper products at home. I ordered premium paper and had to buy ink a couple of times, but we definitely saved a lot of money. We ordered save-the-date postcards to help save on postage. I am so glad we did this because our friends loved our invitations and many of them still have them hanging up on their refrigerators."

HAIR/MAKEUP: Free

"I did my own makeup and a friend who can do retro hairstyling offered to do my hair for the wedding since I wanted a vintage look."

WEDDING PARTY: N/A

WEDDING BANDS: $50

"I still hadn't found the perfect wedding band to fit my engagement ring by the wedding so we opted to borrow my mom's old promise ring for the ceremony and I wore that for about six months until I found the perfect wedding band. Sheldon's band was sterling silver."

COORDINATOR/PLANNER: N/A

"This is one thing I swore I didn't need, and after the wedding I wish I had at least appointed a friend to be my right-hand man during the whole wedding process so I wouldn't be the only person who knew all the details. I still wouldn't want to pay someone for this because I have control issues, but having someone as backup would have helped a lot."

OFFICIANT: Free
(friend of the couple)

"We didn't want an overly religious wedding. We wanted a celebration, so we had a friend officiate the wedding for us. She wrote the most beautiful vows that were spiritual without being heavily religious and it set the tone for the ceremony perfectly. This definitely added to the creative DIY feel that the rest of the wedding had."

LICENSE: $5
(as opposed to $50, since the couple went through premarital counseling, which certain counties reward)

"While this was kind of weird for us, I would recommend it to anyone. We of course went through the counseling for the price break, but we found out a lot of things about each other that we probably wouldn't have talked about if we weren't prompted during our sessions. The counseling sessions were provided by a friend who is also a minister."

OTHER: $640
(party rental, free tent [a friend of the family, the owner of a local car dealership, loaned them the tent for the reception—genius!]; free tables [borrowed from the mom's church])

"Don't be afraid to ask to borrow things you don't have! Use connections. The things we couldn't borrow, we got through a local party rental place."

TOTAL: about $6,165

Under $15K

········· Ila and Hiroki ·········

LOCATION: Costa Mesa, California

GUEST COUNT: 54

VENUES: $500
(ceremony was held at the Santa Ana Courthouse, and reception was held at the Old Vine Café on a Sunday)

FOOD/DRINK: $6,000, plus tax and gratuity

ATTIRE/ACCESSORIES: $520
(bride's dress was a prom dress from Bloomingdale's, $275; bride's shoes, $65; custom fascinator, $40; groom's shoes, $40 [Converse]; cufflinks, $40; tie, $60; jewelry was bride's "something borrowed" and the groom's suit was pre-owned)

FLOWERS: $225
(for two bouquets for parents)

DECOR: $60
(includes baby succulents purchased at the farmer's market, paper for place cards, and little pots that the groom's mother made in pottery class)

DJ/BAND/ENTERTAINMENT: Free
(just an iPod, as the venue was a tiny restaurant)

PHOTOGRAPHY: Free
(Picotte Photography, won through a contest on the Broke-Ass Bride blog! A free photo booth was also gifted by friends.)

VIDEOGRAPHY: N/A

CAKE: Included in the food/drink costs
"We liked the idea of delicious cheesecake that the restaurant had to offer, rather than pretty but bland wedding cakes. It was so good that people asked for seconds!"

FAVORS: $45
(DIY jam made by bride and her sister, yum!)

INVITATIONS/PRINTING/POSTAGE: About $220
(Paper Source paper, designed by bride's sister, printed at home)

HAIR/MAKEUP: Free
(hair was done as a gift by bride's hairstylist, makeup done by bride's mother)

WEDDING PARTY: N/A
"We chose not to have a bridal party, as this was more like a dinner party."

WEDDING BANDS: $2,700
(custom-made by the bride's friends' parents, who are jewelers!)

COORDINATOR/PLANNER:
Free
(barter/friendor combo alert!
A Good Affair, a friend's start-
up coordination company,
donated service in exchange for
experience)

OFFICIANT: N/A
(ceremony performed by Justice
of the Peace at courthouse)

LICENSE: $20

OTHER: $10
(wedding website domain)

TOTAL: $10,300

························· Julie and Scott ············ ··········

LOCATION: Fair Hill, Maryland

GUEST COUNT: 112

VENUE: $300
(The Tea Barn at Fair Hill)
*"$300 for the entire weekend! Woot!
Although the barn took a lot of
sprucing up, I really liked that we
could make it ours and not have a
generic hotel conference room as
our backdrop. The barn was cheap
because it's state owned. Oh, yeah,
and this also led us to start calling
our wedding the 'Hoedown of Love.'"*

FOOD/DRINK: $3,135
*"We spent $2,100 for a wood-fired
pizza food truck. It was delicious
and everyone loved that our caterer
was cooking pizzas in the oven on
the back of a 1950s Ford pickup.
We also chose pizza because it fit
with our laid-back venue, we knew
it would come out hot, and neither
of us ever remembered being wowed
by filet or chicken at other weddings*

*we'd been to. So it was pizza for
the win!*
*"The booze cost about $1,000, and
was a gift from Scott's parents. We
also had friends who brought a few
cases of beer along as a wedding
present. We did three beers, two
wines, and a signature drink—a
spiked cider that we termed
'Hoedown Hooch.' We also had to
acquire a liquor license for $35."*

ATTIRE/ACCESSORIES: $1,610
*"My dress and a sash that I added on
were $1,262. Alterations were $50.
My shoes were $115. (Definitely
a silly splurge in retrospect. They
were gorgeous but uncomfortable as
hell!) My bridal headband was $40,
and tux rental for the groom, plus a
new tie, were $143."*

FLOWERS: $300
*"This was also a gift from Scott's
parents and a family friend, who
had worked as a florist and got the
flowers wholesale."*

(continues)

DECOR: $1,498

"This included a lot of smaller DIY projects. Some of the bigger expenses were fabric for table runners that my mom sewed ($91), votive candles and holders ($178), ribbon for a ribbon curtain ($71), bamboo plates and utensils ($318), tablecloth/napkin rentals ($232), and stemless wine glasses ($240). I know it sounds kind of ridiculous, but I didn't want to rent glassware for a similar price as wholesale and then have our parents need to worry about returning them while we were on our honeymoon. Also, even though it was a broke-ass wedding, I really didn't want people drinking out of Solo cups, and I couldn't find disposable wine cups that I liked.

"I spray-painted empty wine bottles and designed table number labels for them as our centerpieces, which saved a lot of money. They each got a few flowers in them, but not huge bouquets. I also made a ton of those tissue paper pom-poms (which was probably my most-hated project, but it was cheap) and strung up white Christmas lights for atmosphere. I got a bunch of crappy frames from Goodwill, spray-painted them, and painted the glass with chalkboard paint. The various chalkboards served as signage (gifts, menu, guest book, etc.) in the barn.

"The biggest statement was probably the ribbon curtain, which we made to hide the ugly back end of the barn. I also cut a sign out of foam-core that said 'Clearly, this is awesome' (a quote from our second date), which I wrapped in yarn and hung up with the ribbon curtain. I know I sound like an insane crafter (and I am), but it's something I've always been into and as a designer/slight control freak, I really wanted to make our wedding look good despite being on a tight budget."

DJ/BAND/ENTERTAINMENT: $350

"One of our friends is a professional DJ and he worked on the cheap for us."

PHOTOGRAPHY: $1,700

"We got 8 hours of coverage and all the high-res photos but no album. I'm a designer, so designing an album is something I will do for us (someday . . .)."

VIDEOGRAPHY: N/A

"It would have been nice but we didn't really even consider it because we knew there was no room in our budget."

CAKE: $425

"My mom really wanted us to use a specific bakery, which was fine by us because they're reputable and it was one less thing for us to research/decide on."

FAVORS: $111

"We did packets of hot chocolate and marshmallows tied up in cake decorating bags to look like ice cream cones. Another intense DIY project, but I didn't want to give something random or useless, and I figured we couldn't go wrong with food."

INVITATIONS/PRINTING/ POSTAGE: $1,255
(invitations were $1,145, save-the-dates were $110)
"This is the one area where I wanted to go no-holds-barred splurge-tastic. I'm a designer, so I really wanted to do awesome invitations. Obviously with the design fee cut out, and with know-how, I was able to save a lot on printing. Our invitations were a four-page booklet that I did as a two-color job. I got in touch with a letterpress printer whom I'd worked with before and I knew was really reasonable. She did the printing and trimming, but I assembled and bound all the booklets. I printed and cut out envelope liners myself, printed and cut address labels, and got crafty with belly bands and stamps. The same thing went for the save-the-dates, except that I printed them all myself. My only real cost for save-the-dates was ink and postage (and lots of my time)."

HAIR/MAKEUP: $20
"My hair is really short, so I didn't get it done, just put some product and a headband in and called it a day. My makeup was done for free as a courtesy package because my five bridesmaids and mom got their makeup (and their hair) done at the same salon. I guess you could say my makeup cost $20, since that's what I tipped the stylist."

WEDDING PARTY: $260
(gifts for bridesmaids and groomsmen)

WEDDING BANDS: $334

COORDINATOR/PLANNER: N/A
"I delegated tasks (like paying vendors, etc.) to responsible people and gave everyone an information sheet of "really important stuff" and a schedule. I'm sure there were some issues but I didn't have to deal with them, my awesome bridal party and family did! But I also organized and planned everything down to a 'T,' so I think that made it much easier on them."

OFFICIANT: Free (a friend)

LICENSE: $30

OTHER: $295
(hotel room, 2 nights)
"I'm thrifty, but spending the night at my mother-in-law's house the night of my wedding is where I draw the line."

TOTAL: $11,623

LOCATION: Marlborough, New Hampshire

GUEST COUNT: 100

VENUE: $2,500
(Camp Glen Brook)
"Our NH summer camp venue cost $4,000 to rent out for the weekend, minus $1,500 from 50 guests who paid $30 each to stay overnight on Friday and Saturday."

FOOD/DRINK: $4,350
"This cost covered dinner on Friday, all three meals on Saturday, and Sunday brunch. The camp culinary director catered our big meals and we covered the drinks (beer and wine) and lunches with supplies from Trader Joe's, using my sister's employee discount."(Savings savvy alert! Use whatever discounts you have access to.)

ATTIRE/ACCESSORIES: $1,121
"I found my dress on sale at Nordstrom.com (for $44!), my husband bought a suit at J. Crew using his teacher discount, and we both found shoes on sale."

FLOWERS: $200
"We got flowers from local flower farms, and the rest my mom grew in her garden, including the single 12-inch dahlia I carried instead of a full bouquet."

DECOR: $100
"I bought lots of vintage cloth napkins on eBay, made my own tissue paper flag banners, and hung bistro lights in the barn where our ceremony took place."

DJ/BAND/ENTERTAINMENT: Free
"We created a playlist that my father-in-law (who is a professional DJ) played over his sound equipment—we were lucky enough to have him available to take requests."

PHOTOGRAPHY: $2,000
(Maureen Cotton)
"The amazing Boston-based wedding photographer Maureen Cotton gave us a huge 'old friend' discount."

VIDEOGRAPHY: N/A

CAKE: $200
"We also had a make-your-own ice cream sundae bar!"

FAVORS: $40
"I made more than 100 friendship bracelets and we had 1-inch pins created with an image a friend had painted of one of the camp's cabins."

INVITATIONS/PRINTING/ POSTAGE: $40
"Our artist friends designed an invitation for us that we had printed as a postcard at vistaprint .com."

HAIR/MAKEUP: Free
"My sister and sister-in-law took care of this for me."

WEDDING PARTY: $230
"We let our friends and family wear their own clothes, so this cost took care of gifts: I made necklaces for my bridesmaids, and the groomsmen got coolers."

WEDDING BANDS: $340
"We found our rings online on Etsy and on Amazon."

COORDINATOR/PLANNER: N/A

OFFICIANT: Free
"My college roommate performed our ceremony."

LICENSE: $85

OTHER: $118
(for program and thank-you card printing)

TOTAL: $11,324

Under $20K

············ Christen and Leigh ············

LOCATION: Kohala Coast, Hawaii

GUEST COUNT: 50

VENUE: $3,711
(The Mauna Lani Bay Hotel and Bungalows)

FOOD/DRINK: $5,702

ATTIRE/ACCESSORIES: $377
(bride's wedding dress, $196 from David's Bridal; accessories, $85; groom's attire [khaki shorts, such a cute idea!], $96)
"My garter, necklaces, and earrings were all bought from Etsy sellers. I got a Boston Red Sox garter for about $35 and had two strands of turquoise pearl necklaces made to fit around my own pearls for $50. The jewelry designer threw in a pair of earrings for free. We looked for attire that Leigh would wear again—and he did! He lived in the shorts and shoes for the entire summer, so they were a great purchase."

FLOWERS: N/A
(brooch bouquet, assembled by groom's mother)
"All of the brooches were gifted to me, some by my late mother, some by Leigh's mother, others by family and friends. Leigh's mum assembled them all and bought the remaining supplies as a gift to me."

DECOR: $1,877
(tiki torches, Chinese lanterns, lounge chairs; bunting made by groom's mother)
"I wanted color, but didn't want to take away too much from the aesthetic of Hawaii. Leigh's mum made the bunting as a gift, and we rented tiki torches, Chinese lanterns, and a wicker lounge set from the hotel to add to the ambience. The bunting was draped across each table for added color."

DJ/BAND/ENTERTAINMENT: Free
"Leigh and I were very particular about the music we wanted. It wasn't an important facet for our ceremony, so we opted out of having music during that portion. However, for the reception it was entirely necessary. We spent nearly a year compiling some of our and our families' favorite recommendations, putting them in a playlist, and setting the dance floor on fire. We used our laptop as the official emcee of the night."

PHOTOGRAPHY: $4,875
(Persimmon Images; includes $350 discount for finding them on the Broke-Ass Bride blog!)
"We found Kat and Justin through the Broke-Ass Bride and loved their style. I talked to Kat for a while and was able to negotiate a few extra days of shooting, including the

bachelor/bachelorette parties, a trip around the island, and the Fourth of July in exchange for airfare and hotel. I couldn't have been happier."

VIDEOGRAPHY: N/A

CAKE: $325
"Cupcakes, baby! Though we ordered entirely too many. We had about twenty leftover cupcakes to nosh on during the remainder of our stay."

FAVORS: N/A
"I've never taken home a favor from a wedding and put it to use. This being the case, Leigh and I opted out of paying extra money to not only purchase them but also truck them to the island and then burden our guests with bringing them back home."

INVITATIONS/PRINTING/ POSTAGE: Free
(Invitations by Dawn)
"We found amazing (and amazingly cheap!) invitations through Invitations by Dawn. Leigh's mother purchased them as a gift for us."

HAIR/MAKEUP: $225
(Lilikoi Hair Studio)
"I wanted to get all my prettiness done up real good for my wedding day, and this was one area where I was more than willing to splurge."

WEDDING PARTY: $302
"Leigh found pocket watches on Amazon for about $30 each that fit the aesthetic he was going for. I

bought flasks—garter flasks for the girls and a regular flask for my bridesdude. My cousin, who garnered the Junior Bridesmaid title, was adorned with a ring and bracelet from a local jewelry store."

WEDDING BANDS: $52 (Kathryn Riechert)
"We found Kathryn on Etsy. She had a style we liked and a price point to match."

COORDINATOR/PLANNER: See Venue
"Coordination and planning was part of the package deal through the hotel. I worked closely and cohesively with the Mauna Lani's wedding planning staff throughout, long-distance, to ensure everything ran smoothly—and it did!"

OFFICIANT: See Venue
(included in wedding package purchase)
"The officiant's fee was covered in our wedding package purchase."

LICENSE: See Venue
(included in wedding package purchase)

OTHER: $1,000
(airfare)

TOTAL: $18,446

Under $25K

LOCATION: Burlingame, California

GUEST COUNT: 120

VENUE: $14,028
(Crystal Springs Golf Course)

FOOD/DRINK: See Venue
"This was included in our venue fee—we opted for a lower per-person package cost, and added on additional hours of an open bar. In total, we covered the cost of three hours of bar and moved to a cash bar for two hours."

ATTIRE/ACCESSORIES: $1,020
"I snagged my gown from Priscilla of Boston during their going-out-of-business sale for $700, and spent $150 on alterations. I also bought Badgley Mischka shoes from Rue La La online for $50 with tax and shipping. Chris's tux rental was $120."

FLOWERS: $936
"Flowers for the reception were also included in the package. We paid $936 for the bouquets at Rosedale Floral Design—one for the bride and six for the bridesmaids; ten boutonnieres and two corsages for our moms."

DECOR: N/A
"We really didn't do much in terms of decor except add votive candles and little Hershey's Kisses on the table. We had enough children to make a designated kid table. So I went to the local dollar store and grabbed $15 worth of toys and books. It was actually a total hit and hilarious to watch the kids decide who got what."

DJ/BAND/ENTERTAINMENT: See venue
(included in package)

PHOTOGRAPHY: $2,706
(Chasing Glimpses)
"We paid for the 'Kermit and Miss Piggy Package,' which included six hours of photography at the wedding and nearby locations, two photographers, 2,500+ photos, six hours on-site; twenty hours postproduction, seventy-five photos in a modern flush-mount photo album, private sixty-day viewing in an online gallery with sharing and purchasing options, plus a DVD of approximately 500 of the best images of the wedding day. Also, the girls were willing to stay an extra hour with no notice when I realized we hadn't really gotten certain shots during the reception."

VIDEOGRAPHY: N/A
"Didn't do it, but we kind of regret that."

CAKE: See Venue
"The cake was included in our venue package. It was delicious and super-easy to get put together. I e-mailed a photo of the cake design I liked and tried all the combinations. I think Chris liked this part of the planning the best."

FAVORS: $130
"I made our favors. I'm a huge supporter/volunteer of Make-A-Wish. Using scrapbooking paper, I put together little paper favors that asked people to 'Make-A-Wish for the Bride and Groom.' Each had a $1 coin attached. We asked people to either put the coin in a vase near the door or make a larger deposit for Make-A-Wish. In the end, we donated $310 to the Greater Bay Area Chapter."

INVITATIONS/PRINTING/ POSTAGE: $92
"My friend designed the invitations and RSVPs. I work at a newspaper, and after I asked the publisher about a printing contact, he offered to cover the cost as a gift. We spent $92 on postage. Our save-the-date was a video made by a friend who is starting a wedding videography side business."

HAIR/MAKEUP: $120
"A friend who is also starting a business did my hair and makeup. She did a test and also bought new makeup for the wedding day, which I kept for touch-ups."

WEDDING PARTY: $85
"I bought personalized necklaces for the girls on Etsy."

WEDDING BANDS: $600
"We got simple bands, ordered through a family connection who works in the jewelry industry."

COORDINATOR/PLANNER: N/A
(there was an on-site coordinator with the venue, but her involvement didn't extend beyond the actual day-of location specifics)

OFFICIANT: Free
(bride's brother)

LICENSE: $40

OTHER: $325
($15 on treats for the kiddos in attendance; $310 on hotels over two nights)
"We did stay local but wanted to be separate on the day of the wedding. We let our siblings crash at our apartment and stayed at the hotel on our wedding night."

TOTAL: $20,082

Under $30K

····················· Mindy and Tim ·····················

LOCATION: Anaheim, California

GUEST COUNT: 60

VENUE: $2,200
(Disneyland Hotel)
"For our venue, there was a fee for the ceremony spot only. The reception venue was 'free' if you purchased a food and drink minimum, which we did."

FOOD/DRINK: $10,665
"Our cocktail hour was $850. The three-course meal was $6,315, hosted bar for four hours was $3,500, including tax and service charge/tip."

ATTIRE/ACCESSORIES: $1,365
"My dress was $15 at a thrift shop and cost around $400 to alter. My shoes were around $50 and I also bought pink TOMS to change into for the reception at around $40. The veil was DIY for around $30. Necklace was $80. My tiara was a splurge at $250. His suit, including vest rental, was around $400, and shoes were another $100."

FLOWERS: $200
(includes centerpieces and aisle decor)
"I made all the personal floral, aisle arrangements, and centerpieces out of fabric; $200 is the estimated cost of supplies (fabric, floral stems, felt, glue, ribbon) that I acquired over time."

DECOR: $2,500
"We paid around $1,000 for our ceremony decor, which featured fresh floral displays, tulle and bead swagging on the gazebo, and shepherds hook rentals to hang my DIY fabric floral displays. All this was ordered and arranged through Disney. This also included around $550 for Chiavari chairs, $300 for lighting, $400 for specialty chargers, and $250 for specialty linens (tablecloths and napkins)."

DJ/BAND/ENTERTAINMENT: $3,050
"Our DJ was $800, and the character appearances (Mickey, Minnie, and Donald) were $2,250 for all three."

PHOTOGRAPHY: $3,100
(includes videography by a friendor; score!)
"Our photography package was $2,600 (severely discounted because I won an Internet contest), and we paid for our videographer's hotel room and tickets to Disneyland the following day for a total of $500 for our 'free' videography."

VIDEOGRAPHY: N/A

CAKE: $1,300
(three-tier cake with custom design; cost includes the hotel's exclusive white chocolate castle cake topper for $200)

FAVORS: See DJ

"We had a photo booth, which we passed off as our favors; it was a $500 add-on from our DJ."

INVITATIONS/PRINTING/ POSTAGE: $500

"A friend custom made our invitation design (the main invitation and three inserts) for free, which we then had printed at Staples for around $80. We ordered the rest of the supplies from Cards & Pockets for $370 and assembled everything ourselves. We also commissioned another friend to custom make a "storybook" save-the-date announcement for $50, which we had printed online through DocuCopies.com."

HAIR/MAKEUP: $150

(hair was $75 and makeup was $75)

"I received a reduced rate (by half) because I had three other women get hair and makeup services for the event (both moms and my sister-in-law paid for their own hair and makeup at the same rates)."

WEDDING PARTY: $500

"I bought my mom, mom-in-law, sister-in-law, and my two friends who helped plan my shower a Disney wristlet and a necklace as a thank-you gift. My groom bought the dads, brothers, and his two friends who threw his bachelor party an engraved beer mug from Things Remembered."

WEDDING BANDS: $280

"We didn't really consider our rings part of the wedding budget since they were gifts to each other. My engagement ring was $2,900 from Tiffany's, and I picked out a cheap band on Amazon for $30. I also got his band on Amazon for $250."

COORDINATOR/PLANNER: $1,250

(Laura with Rebel Belle Weddings)

OFFICIANT: $30 (friend, ordained online)

"The $30 was for the ordination fee through Rose Ministries."

LICENSE: $90

OTHER: $130

(reception power fee)

"This is a fee Disney charges if you use an 'outside' DJ instead of their in-house DJ (still way cheaper)."

TOTAL: $27,310

LOCATION: Sleepy Hollow, New York

GUEST COUNT: 120

VENUE: $2,800

(Washington Irving's Sunnyside)
"I recommend historic venues that do not see tons of wedding action—they are nearly always cheaper than designed wedding barns, country clubs, or catering halls. The lush ambience of our site was unmatched, as it was right on the Hudson River and guests could explore the grounds, gardens, and Irving's cottage. We also chose to get married in late spring, as everything was gorgeous and green.

"Be wary of sites that come with exclusive caterers, as they can often charge more. We were fortunate in that we got to choose and bring in our own caterer. Venues in the northeast can run you thousands in site fees—some of the cheaper ones I saw were $6,000! It boggled my mind, especially since you have yet to pay for anything else."

FOOD/DRINK: $12,000

(catering by Christine of Fairfield, CT; Town Line Wine, Spirits and Beer of Stratford, CT)
"This amount included all food and drink, and all rentals of tables, chairs, silverware, barware, linens, twinkle lights, serving tables, and the cost of waitstaff, bartenders, and the catering coordinator. They set up and broke down everything, set up the guest and gift tables just

as I envisioned, and even hired someone to hang the chandeliers that I painted and blinged out with crystals.

"The caterer allowed us to bring in our own alcohol, mixers, and ice—purchased wholesale from a great friend who owns a liquor store. He was able to take back what we didn't drink, and was very attentive in helping the caterer run things smoothly. It's a big bonus if you can do the alcohol yourself; that cuts way down on the bar tab. Most caterers charge a ton extra per person for an open bar—upward of $15–$20 per person. I did the math, and our option works out to less than $8 per person for alcohol! Major score."

ATTIRE/ACCESSORIES: $970

(The bride snagged her custom dress and sash from Dolly Couture for $700; the groom's tux was free from Men's Warehouse with the groomsmen's' tux rentals)
"To me, it made no sense to try on gowns that were not in my size, had to be held on with those orange binder clips, and mostly did not have straps. The girls are DDs and need a bra to hold them up! I wasn't going to worry about them flying out during 'Moves Like Jagger' to the horror of all. Also, you must order boutique dresses to fit your widest point and then the seamstress has to alter the hell out of it to make it fit the rest of your body, often adding hundreds of $$$ to the dress

bill. I needed to find a dress that came in a 'long' length since I would be a tad over 6 feet tall in my heels.

"One of my bridesmaids, bless her heart, saw me growing sad at not being able to find a dress I liked and suggested that I 'get a short dress and rock a hot pair of shoes.' She was a genius—when I Googled 'short wedding dresses,' Dolly's site immediately came up. I fell in love with her retro aesthetic and high-quality materials. I got measured at the bridal shop where my 'maids bought their dresses, sent the numbers to Nickie and Dolly, and they got to work designing my dress.

"I was able to have the sort of details that would have cost hundreds or thousands otherwise— peach satin ribbon sewn into the petticoat, a scalloped edge, and a sweetheart neckline (with straps!). I chose all the fabric myself, from samples they sent me in the mail. I wore my favorite bra on the day of the wedding, and didn't need any shapewear to look fabulous—Dolly's dress did all the work. Her prices are fantastically reasonable, and the customer service is top-notch.

"I did not want a veil, so I chose a peach hair flower from Etsy (about $15). I picked up my faux-pearl-and-amber-crystal earrings for a song from a local boutique, and my beautiful cameo was a gift from my bridesmaids. I wore a bracelet from my mom, used her white vintage beaded clutch from the '60s, and my maid of honor gifted me my 'something blue'—my garter, which had blue fabric flowers (she also purchased it from Etsy).

"My shoes were my big expense— they are from the Butter label, and cost around $200. Since I was wearing a short dress, my shoes mattered to me so everyone could admire them all day. I custom dyed my shoes ($20) at the cobbler I always go to when I need a shoe repair or polish, and got the clip-on shoe flowers in a matching peach hue on Etsy for $30. Jay's accessories were minimal: cuff links I'd gotten for him for a previous anniversary, and a $15 cream-colored tie from Tie Bar to match my dress."

FLOWERS: $1,500
(Port Chester Florist)
"This is what I paid for a bridal bouquet, 6 bridesmaid bouquets, 2 mother and 1 grandmother corsages, 10 bouts for the guys and dads, arrangements for 7 tables, 6 pew flower baskets, 2 altar arrangements, greens for the tent, and miscellaneous small single-stem arrangements for guest, gift, and dessert tables. I did not have my heart set on any one flower, which made the budgeting process easier for the florist."

DECOR: $800
"Since the tent at Sunnyside was bare-bones, I needed to make it look fancy all by myself. I scored nearly all of my decor from Save On Crafts, Etsy, HomeGoods, or from brides on the Weddingbee Classifieds. (I first discovered Dana via Weddingbee!)"

(continues)

DJ/BAND/ENTERTAINMENT:
$1,000

PHOTOGRAPHY: $2,500
(Christopher Schmelke
Photography)
*"I had met Christopher at an event
and discovered he was a wedding
photographer. I looked at the
portfolios of photographers at a
wide range of price points, and
found Christopher's work was more
intimate and really captured both
the emotions and the details of the
weddings."*

VIDEOGRAPHY: N/A

CAKE: $400
(Cupcakes by Missy of
White Plains, NY)
*"We did cupcakes for the guests, and
a giant cupcake served as our 'cake
to cut.' It was just large enough to
hold our custom geeky cake topper
(from an Etsy seller)—me in a
Starfleet uniform and Jay in a Han
Solo outfit!"*

FAVORS: $200
*"I got small glass jars from a
wholesale bottle company ($60 for
150), and tied ribbons and favor
tags (stickers from Etsy) to them.
The day before the wedding, we
picked up assorted cookies from
a bakery down the street—about
a hundred dollars' worth—and
filled the cookie jars. Our guests
appreciated the take-home treat,
and I've seen the small jars in my
friends' houses, holding everything
from paper clips to makeup brushes.
Useful and tasty!"*

**INVITATIONS/PRINTING/
POSTAGE:** $375
*"This is an area I'm proud of! My
brother is very artistic and drew
our invites as a gift to us—he did
the invitation itself, plus additional
designs on the direction RSVP cards.*

*"I ordered all our paper wholesale
from PaperandMore.com ($175)
and had a bunch leftover to make
cute signs for the cupcake flavors
and other things. A nearby printer
scanned my brother's drawings,
helped me choose a font, and
printed and cut everything for the
reasonable price of $100.*

*"I picked up some clear address
labels at Staples, imported all
our addresses onto the correct size
template in Word, and printed them
on our home computer. I borrowed
the printer's fancy glue-tape gun
and assembled the invites with a
friend. It took practically no time at
all and was extra easy!"*

HAIR/MAKEUP: $75
*"Makeup was free, and done by
a good friend with experience in
the showbiz/modeling industry.
Hair was done at Eclipse salon in
Tarrytown."*

WEDDING PARTY: $60
*"I gifted my girls earrings from Etsy
($10 per pair), which they wore
on the day of the wedding. Jay
chose to give his groomsmen nifty
Transformer USB drives, each with a
custom playlist. He used a gift card
from the points he had accumulated
on his credit card to purchase them
from Amazon."*

WEDDING BANDS: $300

COORDINATOR/PLANNER:
N/A

"I coordinated and planned the entire weekend, and my friend Rob (he is mad organized) helped out the day of, making sure the proverbial trains ran on time. I was day-of coordinator for another friend the previous year—so just pick someone you trust and ask. Chances are, their type-A personality will jump for organizational joy!"

OFFICIANT: $700 (with tip)

"We were married in a church ($500 fee), and our priest did not specify a donation. We gifted him $200."

LICENSE: $40

OTHER: $1,750

"Transportation was $1,600 for one stretch limo and one Princess Rolls-Royce, paid for by family as a gift to us. Vintage umbrella rentals from Bella Umbrella for the bridesmaids (made for awesome photos) were $150."

TOTAL: $25,470

Over $30K

LOCATION: Polebridge, Montana

GUEST COUNT: 100

VENUE: $500

"We were married in a field in a small town in Montana, and this fee reserved that space and the nearby stage and seating for our wedding. This $500 was solely for permission to use the area and the guarantee that there wouldn't be another event going on."

FOOD/DRINK: $4,400

"All-inclusive of our delicious pizza rehearsal dinner, a half-keg of beer, wine and Champagne, cocktail mixers (a friend provided infusions and bartending as a gift), cocktail-hour hors d'oeuvres, and a full dinner with locally sourced and organic ingredients. Yum!"

ATTIRE/ACCESSORIES: $5,050

"He had a custom suit made at a local tailor, which was his big splurge. He also picked up a nice tie and a new dress shirt. However, he gets to wear that suit all the time, still, years later.

"I fell in love with a Pronovias dress ($1,500) after looking long and hard for something that wouldn't be too much for a Montana wedding. After alterations, kick-ass cowboy boots, a veil, and accessories and adornments, my couture collection was embarrassingly expensive. A long engagement gave me ample excuse to keep collecting things that I thought I'd want to wear on our wedding day. I sold most of the accessories after the fact."

FLOWERS: $1,500

"Our flowers included a bridal bouquet and small tossing bouquet, bridesmaids' bouquets, boutonnieres for the guys and for the parents, loose flowers for the ceremony and cocktail hour, and table arrangements for the reception. We saved by having uncut dahlias arranged on the day of by our planner, and simple centerpieces in Mason jars with flowers, grasses, and raffia."

DECOR: $200

"Some of our rustic decor was made by friends and the rest I sourced from craft stores, antique shops, and street markets. We kept it simple because the real beauty was provided by the backdrop against which our wedding was set."

DJ/BAND/ENTERTAINMENT: $1,200

"We hired an amazing bluegrass band from the area, Good Wood. They played acoustic music for our cocktail hour and three hours of sweet tunes on stage after dinner. They made our wedding the memorable celebration that it was and were absolutely worth their weight in gold."

PHOTOGRAPHY: $3,500

"I am a firm believer in hiring a seasoned, qualified professional to preserve wedding memories. Our photographer took our engagement photographs during our summer visit to Montana the year before our wedding. We loved her, so we hired her immediately despite the fact that her prices were about $1,000 over what we were expecting. Some things are worth the investment—after everything else is gone, our photos are what allow us to relive the celebration with friends and family, and feel the joy of the day one more time."

VIDEOGRAPHY: N/A

CAKE: $500

"Our delicious huckleberry buttercream wedding cake and huckleberry/cherry pies were made by the famous Mercantile bakery in Polebridge. It might not have been a sculptural masterpiece of fondant, but I guarantee that it was some of the best damn wedding cake our guests had ever tasted!"

FAVORS: $100

"Favors were also made by the Polebridge Mercantile bakery and assembled by us during the rehearsal dinner—glassine bags with three yummy cookies tied with raffia and a thank-you tag."

INVITATIONS/PRINTING/ POSTAGE: $1,600

"A family friend made our save-the-date cards with photographs from our engagement. Our invitations were another splurge: I drool over letterpress, and a college friend offered her small card studio as the testing ground for her first-ever wedding suite. So, we went a bit overboard and made insanely awesome wedding invitations. All things considered, they were a steal for the amazing works of art that we received, but still spendy for something that just gets recycled anyway."

HAIR/MAKEUP: $155

"Included pre-wedding makeup purchases, a rehearsal-day mani-pedi, a classic up-do for me, and travel for hairstylists from town to the lodge (a 45-minute trip). After a few disappointing makeup trials, I decided to invest the money I'd spend on makeup in purchasing a new kit and doing it myself. I'm picky, so I'm glad I did, despite the added stress."

WEDDING PARTY: $600

"Bridesmaid gifts were handmade jewelry, pashminas, and ceramic birds. Groomsmen gifts were Chambriard pocketknives."

WEDDING BANDS: $3,800

"Yet another splurge. We felt that we wanted to go all out on the symbols of our commitment. He designed a one-of-a-kind platinum and diamond engagement ring at a local jeweler and we worked together to create a wedding band that meshed with it.

"We originally thought he'd get an affordable, rough-and-tumble tungsten carbide wedding band

(continues)

that would outlast his rock climbing. However, he fell in love instead with a platinum and gold number, and I had guilt pangs about not getting him his favorite, so I gave in. C'est la vie."

COORDINATOR/PLANNER: $6,700

"For me, this is where things got a bit financially out of control. I hired our coordinator for full-service planning because I couldn't stomach the thought of pulling together a wedding out of state on my lunch breaks. Her advice on which vendors to use and her ability to contact them, negotiate on our behalf, and set up appointments was invaluable. But ultimately, the feedback I received from online wedding blogs and communities shaped the style and direction of our wedding the most. I think that if I had felt more confident, a different level of planning and consultation would have been sufficient—like month-of planning with day-of coordination.

"Having the planner and her team there on the day of our wedding was absolutely worth it—everything was executed flawlessly, including the hours of setup and tear-down that we didn't have to burden our already-stressed families with, and we felt so well taken care of. Ultimately, having a planner was really worth it for the load off our minds, but I think we could have scaled down on the level of service we purchased."

OFFICIANT: Free

"In Montana, anyone can marry you, even the non-ordained! We had a well-spoken family member tie the knot for us. We wrote our own ceremony and vows using Judith Johnson's book The Wedding Ceremony Planner (along with help from Google) and our 'officiant' friend added her own marriage address."

LICENSE: $55

OTHER: $4,970
(transportation, $370; rentals [chairs, tables, linens, tent], $4,400; miscellaneous, $200)
"Transportation was two school buses, for us, our attendants, and guests. Beep, beep!"

TOTAL: about $35,000

NOTE: Kat had a budget of 24K, but ended up blowing it by 11K, completely by accident. Be advised, BABs! That's the rabbit hole we discussed earlier!

what have we learned here?

One thing almost all of these weddings have in common is the use of community to accomplish more budget-friendly events. From having a sewing machine maven for a mother, to dads who can man a barbecue, to friends who have a knack for florals, utilizing the talent around you can save big bucks.

Many of these couples also chose to forgo favors, which have a tendency to get tossed, or did simple DIY ones instead, saving beaucoup bucks.

The power of negotiation was strong with these young Jedis, and allowed them to have more luxury than they could normally afford. And hunting down contests and discounts through blogs (like mine) saved some of these couples thousands of dollars on services like photography, which is usually one of the biggest-ticket items!

Note that some of the gals who used minimal assistance with coordination had wished for even more in retrospect. I just want to reiterate how essential I feel it is to delegate, or better yet, hire someone to run the show so you don't have to worry about the details or timeline during your own wedding. Professionals know what exactly to plan and look out for, giving them a leg up on the alternative of just asking a responsible friend to oversee things.

I hope these sample budgets were not only helpful in getting a handle on various ways to divide your budget based on priority, clever approaches to savings, great places to shop for deals, and how pricing can vary based on region, but they were also liberating in seeing how couples exercise flexibility about where and how they spend their wedding money, in direct defiance of "the rules." From having a Disney destination to a prairie hootenanny to a restaurant dinner party, each couple sang their own song, spent from the heart, and had the times of their lives!

Recipes

FOR HAPPY BELLIES
AND FULL WALLETS

I absolutely love to cook, and to host dinners and parties for my friends. There's something so special about the intimacy of knowing that everything was made with love. Home-prepped meals can also be a huge money-saving move for engagement parties, rehearsal dinners, and showers, rather than renting out space in restaurants or hiring caterers. It's a special treat to share some of my tried-and-true friends-and-family recipes that are big on taste but low on cost. I hope you love them as much as we do!

> NOTE: If you're self-catering your wedding with the help of friends and family, get as much prep work done a day or two ahead of time, such as chopping vegetables, making sauces that can be reheated later, or cooking rice that can later be gently reheated with a bit of steam and fluffing before being added to a dish.

> BONUS: You can carry these over for any parties or events you host in your newly wedded life!

Beverages for Grown-ups

Broke-Ass Sangria

Hunter invented this sangria for our popular house parties. It couldn't be cheaper or easier to make in large batches for a huge crowd, and it's surprisingly tasty! Try this for your Spanish or Italian feasts, or any fête! **MAKES 25**

> **1 jug (1.5 liter) Carlo Rossi sangria-flavored wine**
> **1 carton orange juice (medium pulp suggested)**
> **½ bottle (750 milliliter) brandy (whatever's cheapest)**
> **2 to 3 cups granulated sugar**
> **Slices of orange, lemon, and lime, cut into rounds**
> **Ice cubes**

1. Mix the wine, juice, brandy, and 2 cups sugar in a large jug or bucket, stirring until the sugar is completely dissolved. Taste for sweetness and add more sugar if desired.

2. Transfer to a tapped beverage jug or soak the label off the Rossi and funnel the sangria into that for serving, reserving any overflow in a pitcher in the refrigerator for easy refills later.

3. Drop in the fruit slices and serve over ice.

4. Get crunk!

Muchas Margaritas!

No fiesta, Mexican or not, is complete without the tangy taste of tequila and lime juice in one of my favorite adult beverages. Now, generally, I tend to be a bit of a purist when it comes to mixing the margs, but for a large group, I prefer an easier, cheaper cheat. I'll give you both versions, for you to use as you see fit!

FRUGAL FAUX-GARITAS MAKES 24

8 cups cold water

1 liter (1⅓ 750-milliliter bottles) tequila, chilled

2 cans (12 ounces each) frozen limeade concentrate, thawed in the refrigerator

½ cup frozen orange juice concentrate, thawed in the refrigerator (about ¾ of a 12-ounce can)

2 cans (12 ounces each) light beer

Ice cubes (optional)

4 large limes, sliced into 6 wedges each

Coarse salt, for rimming the glasses (optional)

1. Mix the water, tequila, limeade and orange juice concentrates, and beer in a large pitcher. Stir well to combine.

2. Serve over ice, with a lime wedge on the rim of each glass.

3. To salt the rims of the glasses, if desired, swipe the lime wedge around each rim, then dip glasses gently into a plate of salt. Shake off the excess, then fill the glasses with ice and the margarita.

MASTERFUL MARGARITAS (ADAPTED FROM RICK BAYLESS)

Chicago-based celebrity chef Rick Bayless has been my culinary hero ever since I fell in love with his PBS cooking show *Mexico: One Plate at a Time*, back in Chicago more than ten years ago. His recipes are to die for, and his demeanor is so mesmerizingly warm and enthusiastic. He and his food are simply addictive. This is a spin on his large-batch margarita that's sure to please even the most discerning palate at your party. **MAKES ROUGHLY 2 DOZEN**

> **1 bottle (750 milliliters) silver or gold tequila (go for 100 percent agave in this sucker; it really makes a difference)**
>
> **1 to 2 cups triple sec, Cointreau, or Grand Marnier (choose your secondary liquor based on how "orange-y" you want your margaritas to taste; triple sec is the least intense, Grand Marnier the most)**
>
> **1 cup fresh lime juice**
>
> **Ice cubes**
>
> **4 large limes, sliced into 6 wedges each**
>
> **Coarse salt, for rimming the glasses (optional)**

1. Mix the tequila with 1 cup of the liqueur and the lime juice in a large pitcher. Taste, and add more liqueur as necessary.

2. Add the ice to glasses just as the drink is being served, add the margarita, and garnish each with a lime wedge on the rim.

3. To salt the rims of the glasses, if desired, swipe the lime wedge around each rim, then dip glasses gently into a plate of salt. Shake off the excess, then fill the glasses with ice and the margarita.

4. *¡Olé!*

Recipes That Rock

. . . .

Since themes play so crucial a role in party planning, I've opted to orga-nize the food recipes by ethnic origin. Feel free to mix and match as you see fit, and make an international feast with something for everyone!

Mama's Pasghetti

This is my mother's famous spaghetti recipe! It could not be easier or yummier, and it gets better the longer it sits and the flavors marry (har, har), so making it a day or two ahead and then reheating it on the day of your event is not only a cinch but also works in your favor!   **SERVES 8**

> 1½ teaspoons olive oil, plus more for the pot
>
> 1 to 2 pounds Italian sausages, casings removed
>
> 1 pound country pork ribs, on the bone
>
> 2 cans (28 ounces each) Italian plum or diced tomatoes
>
> 2 cans (6 ounces each) tomato paste 2 handfuls dried oregano
>
> 1 handful dried basil
>
> 5 or more large heads of garlic, cloves separated, peeled, and crushed
>
> ¾ cup chicken broth
>
> ½ cup red wine, or more to taste
>
> ¾ cup grated or shredded parmesan cheese, plus additional for garnish (optional)
>
> 2 pinches of sugar
>
> Salt and freshly ground pepper
>
> 2 packages (1 pound each) spaghetti
>
> Fresh basil (for garnish; optional)

1. Heat ¼ inch of the oil in the bottom of a large, heavy-bottomed pot over medium heat. When the oil is shimmering, add the sausage and pork, and sear until browned on all sides, 3 to 5 minutes.

2. Add the tomatoes, tomato paste, oregano, basil, garlic, broth, wine, parmesan cheese, 1 pinch of sugar, the 1½ teaspoons oil, and 2 tomato-paste cans of water. Stir until combined.

3. Reduce the heat to low and simmer gently for 2 hours, stirring occasionally.

4. Taste, and add the remaining pinch of sugar if the sauce is too acidic. Add salt and pepper to taste. If you're making the sauce ahead of time, store it in the refrigerator.

5. When ready to serve, cook the pasta in boiling, heavily salted water for 8 minutes or until al dente. Rinse the pasta under cold water to prevent overcooking, reserving a cup of the cooking liquid; add a ladleful or two of the sauce to the pasta to prevent the noodles from sticking together.

6. If you made the sauce ahead of time and have chilled it, stir the reserved pasta water into your sauce as you reheat it.

7. Remove the meat and serve alongside the pasta and sauce in separate bowls, allowing your guests to customize their portions. If desired, garnish servings with additional parmesan cheese and snipped fresh basil, and serve with a large salad, crusty bread, and herbed butter (recipe follows).

(continues)

HERBED BUTTER SERVES 14 TO 16

8 ounces unsalted butter, at room temperature

¼ teaspoon minced fresh garlic

1 tablespoon minced fresh parsley

1 tablespoon minced fresh basil

1 teaspoon fresh lemon juice

1 teaspoon kosher or coarse sea salt

½ teaspoon freshly ground pepper

1. Combine the butter, garlic, parsley, basil, lemon juice, salt, and pepper by gently beating at medium speed in a mixer until blended—do not whip.

2. Pack the herbed butter into baby-food jars and refrigerate until ready to use. Just before serving, take the jars out of the refrigerator and allow to come to room temperature. Alternatively, form the butter into a log in the center of a large sheet of plastic wrap, and refrigerate (or freeze) until hard enough to slice into rounds for individual servings.

Greek Avgolemono Soup

My grandmother hailed from Greece, and one of my favorite family traditions happens on Easter, when my father cooks a huge Greek feast for the family. This recipe for traditional avgolemono (egg-lemon) soup is a comforting, delicious family staple and is also perfect for a crowd! **SERVES 8**

> **1 cup white rice**
>
> **4 cans (14 ounces each) chicken broth or 8 cups homemade chicken stock**
>
> **2 large eggs**
>
> **2 lemons, zested and juiced**

1. Cook the rice according to the package directions and set aside.

2. Bring the broth to a simmer in a large stockpot over low-medium heat and add the rice.

3. Using a hand mixer at medium speed, beat the eggs in a large, heat-friendly bowl until they are very frothy. Add the juice and zest, and beat a little longer to combine the ingredients and aerate the mixture.

4. Slowly ladle ½ cup to 1 cup of hot broth into the egg mixture, while continuously beating, to temper the eggs. Add the egg mixture to the stockpot, stirring well. Remove pot from the heat (do not continue to cook the soup, or else the eggs will curdle). Serve immediately.

5. If you must hold over the soup, keep it warm in a double boiler or set the pot over another pot filled with hot water.

A Mexican Fiesta Buffet Bar

Awhile back, I threw a friend a surprise party and created a "make your own nachos or burrito" buffet to add a fun, interactive dynamic to the bash. It packs a lot of visual and filling punch for what is a relatively simple and affordable group meal to assemble! The ingredients are all low cost and bulk friendly, so shop at a local warehouse grocer, such as Costco or Sam's Club, if you can, and don't be daunted by the long list of ingredients. Once you have everything you need, it's mostly a matter of some light cooking or chopping and arranging. I keep the buffet vegetarian for added simplicity and broader appeal, but feel free to sauté some beef or chicken with taco seasoning for a heartier offering. And that *queso*! I swear, it's the easiest thing ever. (And, sure, Velveeta is not the world's classiest cheese, but people go NUTS for it!) I famously make this for every party I throw, and the one time I skipped it, a friend joked that he was leaving because the *queso* was all he came for in the first place.   **MAKES 8 TO 12 SERVINGS**

FOR THE SPANISH RICE
2 tablespoons olive oil

2 tablespoons chopped white onion (see Note 1)

1½ cups Arborio rice

2 cups water or vegetable broth

1 cup chunky salsa

FOR THE QUESO (OF THE GODS)
2 bricks (2 pounds each) Velveeta cheese, cubed

2 cans (14.5 ounces each) diced tomatoes with green chiles (I prefer RoTel brand)

2 cans (10 ounces each) condensed cream of mushroom soup

2 packages (8 ounces each) cream cheese

Hot sauce or cayenne pepper (optional)

FOR THE HOLY GUACAMOLE
¾ cup cold water

¼ cup apple cider vinegar

2 medium white onions, finely chopped

6 large, ripe Haas avocados, halved and pitted, with pits reserved

3 large tomatoes, seeded and chopped

2 to 3 serrano chiles, finely chopped (remove seeds for milder heat; see Note 2)

1 large bunch fresh cilantro, chopped

½ cup fresh lemon or lime juice

Salt and pepper to taste

15 soft flour tortillas

15 soft corn tortillas

3 large bags (24 ounces each) store-bought tortilla chips or 3 batches Fancified Tortilla Chips (recipe follows)

3 cans (32 ounces each) black beans, in their liquid

FOR THE GARNISHES
3 large bunches fresh cilantro, chopped

3 jars salsa (one red, one green, one pico de gallo)

1 tub (32 ounces) sour cream

1 medium head green cabbage, shredded

1 large jar (12 ounces) pickled jalapeños, drained

TO MAKE THE RICE

Heat the oil in a large, heavy skillet over medium heat. Stir in the onion, and cook until transparent, about 5 minutes. Add the rice, stirring often. When the rice begins to brown, stir in the water and salsa. Reduce the heat to low, cover, and simmer for 20 minutes, or until all the liquid has been absorbed. Keep warm, or plan on reheating 30 minutes before serving.

TO MAKE THE QUESO (OF THE GODS)

1. Place the cheese cubes, tomatoes, soup, and cream cheese in a large saucepan. Cover and heat over medium, stirring often to prevent the bottom from burning, until cheese is completely melted and blended with other ingredients, 20 to 30 minutes. Transfer to a

(continues)

slow cooker to keep warm. (If necessary, this can be prepared in a slow cooker from the start, but allow at least 1 hour.)

2. When ready to serve, taste and add hot sauce or cayenne, if desired. (It's best when served immediately, but reduce the heat to low for serving and keep covered when not in use, to prevent skin from forming.)

TO MAKE THE HOLY GUACAMOLE

1. In a medium bowl, combine the water and vinegar, and add the onions to soak while you prepare the rest.

2. Scoop the avocado meat into a large bowl with a spoon, and use a fork to mash it until it's mostly smooth but some small chunks remain. Gently fold in the tomatoes, chiles, cilantro, and lemon juice. Drain the onions and fold them in, too. Season to taste with salt and pepper. Place the pits into the guacamole, and/or cover the guacamole with plastic wrap (pushing the wrap down onto its surface) to prevent browning. Refrigerate until ready to serve.

TO ASSEMBLE THE NACHO/BURRITO BAR

1. Lay out the soft tortillas on a platter and place the chips in a large bowl. Warm the beans and reheat the rice in separate baking dishes in a 250°F oven for 30 minutes.

2. When ready to serve, spoon the rice and beans separately into large bowls or disposable metal roasting pans. Set out the queso, either in a bowl or in a slow cooker kept on low (which helps it stay warm), and the bowl of refrigerated guacamole.

3. Put each garnish in its own bowl, and let the guests build their own meals as they choose!

> NOTE 1: *Place a burning candle near your chopping space and chew gum while you chop the onions to prevent onion-cutting tears!*
>
> NOTE 2: *Be careful when handling chiles; serrano oils can irritate your skin, so wear gloves if possible and take care not to touch your mouth, nose, or eyes.*

FANCIFIED TORTILLA CHIPS

For all you overachievers out there, this is my favorite trick (thanks again for the inspiration, Rick Bayless!) for taking a simple chips, salsa, and guacamole appetizer a step beyond the rest. Use your favorite jarred salsas and the guacamole recipe on page 225, and watch your friends go wild asking for your secret! **MAKES 8 TO 9 SNACK SERVINGS**

> ¼ cup vegetable oil
>
> 6 garlic cloves, chopped
>
> 1½ teaspoons freshly ground black pepper, or to taste
>
> 1 large bag (24 ounces) tortilla chips
>
> Kosher salt

1. Preheat the oven to 350°F.

2. Heat the oil in a small saucepan over medium-low heat. Add the garlic and 1 teaspoon of pepper. Heat until the garlic starts to brown, about 10 minutes, taking care not to let it burn. Strain and reserve the oil, and discard the garlic.

3. Spread a single layer of chips on a baking sheet and brush the oil over them, trying to get a little bit on each chip, and lightly salt. Repeat with a second layer, or a second pan, if necessary.

4. Bake for 10 to 12 minutes, or until the edges of the chips are just barely starting to toast. Sprinkle with salt and the remaining pepper. Let cool and serve.

Japanese Roll-Your-Own Sushi Bar

Can you tell yet that I'm a huge sucker for interactive dining experiences? This is a great idea for engagement parties or bridal shower meals that get the guests involved and allow them to eat exactly what they want. This meal can become pricey easily, depending on how far you want to take it, so feel free to make it a potluck experience: assign each guest a filling to bring for the group! The recipe here serves six, so multiply the ingredients as necessary for the size of your crowd. **SERVES 6**

SUPPLIES
Rice cooker

Chopsticks

Sushi rolling mats

Small dishes

FOR THE SUSHI
2 cups sushi rice

2 large, ripe Haas avocados, halved, pitted, peeled, and sliced

1 hothouse or English cucumber, peeled and sliced into matchsticks

½ medium daikon , peeled and sliced into matchsticks

½ cup carrot, peeled and sliced into matchsticks, blanched, and cooled

1 package (6 sheets) nori

1 tub (13.5 ounces) soft cream cheese

2 cups prepared Spicy Tuna (recipe follows)

2 packages (8 ounces each) smoked salmon

Sashimi-grade tuna or salmon, thinly sliced (optional)

1 cup soy sauce or tamari

1 tube wasabi paste

1 cup pickled ginger

TO MAKE THE SUSHI

1. Cook the sushi rice according to the rice cooker instructions, and allow it to cool.

2. Prepare the vegetables as directed.

3. Make the Spicy Tuna.

TO ASSEMBLE THE SUSHI BAR

1. Arrange the cooked rice, sliced vegetables, nori, cream cheese, spicy tuna, smoked salmon, and sashimi-grade tuna (if desired) in bowls and on platters.

2. Put out the sushi rolling mats, chopsticks, and small dishes of soy sauce, wasabi, and ginger.

3. Allow guests to create their own sushi masterpieces!

> *Hint: If your guests seem unsure about making the rolls, encourage them instead to roll the nori into a cone and fill it for a Japanese hand roll, or provide bowls for them to pile with rice, fillings, and toppings instead.*

SPICY TUNA

2 cans (5 ounces each) chunk white albacore tuna, drained and flaked

4 tablespoons mayonnaise

2 to 4 tablespoons Sriracha sauce

In a medium-size bowl, mix the tuna, mayonnaise, and 2 tablespoons of the Sriracha. Taste for heat and add more Sriracha as desired. Refrigerate until ready to use.

How to Feed 40 People for $3 Each

(BY DAFFODIL CAMPBELL)

Last year we celebrated our wedding anniversary with a group of friends. I had considered having the dinner catered, or picking up trays of food from our local grocery store and saving myself a lot of time and stress. But the prices were high, and I wanted the food to be hot and fresh. Besides, I love to cook.

The response from friends on hearing that I was cooking for about forty people on my anniversary ranged from "You ARE?" to "Are you sure?" to "Of course you are!" to "I am so glad you are. Yummy!"

Inspired and wanting to rise to the challenge, I sat down with my cookbooks, looking for recipes that were simple. The more ingredients a recipe has, the more it would cost to make. A tip: If you need a spice or other ingredient that you don't use often, find a store that sells spices by weight. Lots of health food stores do, and you can buy just what you need for the recipe, not a whole jar that will then sit in your pantry.

Also, I have a limited diet these days, so I was hyper-aware of this, but it's a good thing to remember: you want to make something everyone will be able to eat. I decided on a big salad, daal, rice (all vegetarian and very filling, with plant-based protein), and chicken.

I started cooking that afternoon, and it took me about two hours. I had hoped to let the chicken marinate overnight, but it just didn't work out that way, so I put the chicken on the grill to start them off and add some smoky flavor, then stabbed them repeatedly with a fork (which also helped my stress about cooking for forty people, since I was feeling kind of stabby by about 4 p.m.), basted, and cooked them on low heat in my convection oven to allow the flavors to develop slowly.

A caveat about cooking for a large group: *You need big pans.* Big ones. And big serving dishes. And a lot of silverware and plates. We discovered that we needed more forks about an hour before the guests started to arrive.

Awesome. Added to the stabby vibe.

The following is a detailed description of the menu, with some overly simple directions.

The Salad Station

I decided to do the setup as a salad bar. This meant that leftover greens could be bagged and refrigerated, along with the individual garnishes, for reuse. No dressing? *No problem.* Hate carrots? *Hey, me too.*

FOR THE SALAD

3 pounds baby greens (or bite-size romaine)

1 cup dried cranberries

2 cans (11 ounces each) mandarin oranges, drained

½ cup sunflower seeds

2 cucumbers, sliced

2 cups alfalfa sprouts

1 log (12 ounces) goat cheese (chèvre)

5 medium carrots, peeled and grated

1 loaf crusty French bread (better than croutons!), torn into bite-size chunks

FOR THE BALSAMIC STRAWBERRY VINAIGRETTE

½ cup ripe strawberries

½ cup balsamic vinegar

¾ cup olive oil

TO MAKE THE SALAD

In a large bowl, mix all of the ingredients together and set aside.

TO MAKE THE BALSAMIC STRAWBERRY VINAIGRETTE

I am embarrassed to even call this a recipe, actually. I chopped some overly ripe, slightly wrinkly strawberries I had in the kitchen into small pieces, put them in a bowl with their juices, poured in enough balsamic vinegar to cover them, stirred enthusiastically, and then let them sit until the party (about an hour). Just before serving, I added the oil and gave it all a good mixing. That's it! Also great with blueberries. The trick is to use a very sweet, juicy, extra-ripe fruit.

The Rice

Public Service Announcement: *Instant rice is not rice.*

For dinner, I made a huge pot of rice. There is a trick to making rice if you don't have a rice cooker. If you live in Hawaii, as I do, you know what a rice cooker is because almost every household has one. I learned about rice cookers when I moved to Maui. They are like slow cookers, but for rice. They cook rice quickly and efficiently, without scorching, and have an automatic shut-off when the rice is done. I don't know how they work exactly, but we'll just call it a miracle and move on. As a born and bred New Englander with limited storage space, I don't have a rice cooker. I make my rice in a big pot.

The basic rule of thumb for cooking rice is simple: one part rice, two parts water. Always put twice as much water as rice, and you will be fine. However, I have ruined many a pot of rice in my day, and I learned this stress-free trick to making rice if you don't have a rice cooker. Confession: this technique for cooking rice was taught to me by my friend Kevin Flaherty during the middle of a very memorable weekend at his parents' beach house, off-season.

2 tablespoons unsalted butter or 2 tablespoons vegetable or olive oil

8 cups white rice

1. Melt the butter in the bottom of a large pan or stockpot over low heat. Make sure the bottom of the pan is fully coated.

2. Wash and drain the rice. Just do it.

3. Pour the rice into the pan. *Do not stir.*

4. Pour 4 quarts of cold water over the rice, and turn the heat to high. When the water comes to a boil, put on the lid and turn the heat down to low, simmering until the water is absorbed, 18 to 25 minutes.

   NOTE: You cannot put the lid on tightly; if you want to use a lid, it has to be slightly off-center so the steam can escape, and you have to keep an eye on the pan. Once the water is gone, you must turn off the heat or your rice will burn! It's easy to tell when the water is completely gone: look for bubbles on top of and between the grains of rice. Bubbles = water still cooking off.

Daal/Dal/Dhal (aka Lentils)

My friend Sarala, who has lived and studied in India, taught me all about making daal. The thing about daal is that you can make it many different ways—it can be very spicy or mild and the consistency can vary from sort of watery to thick and creamy. Just remember: it's hard to screw it up, and you can add water as needed if it gets too thick. The original recipe makes enough for ten people, so I quadrupled it for my party. **MAKES 10 SERVINGS**

¾ cup (1½ sticks) unsalted butter or ghee

4 large yellow onions, chopped

¼ cup minced fresh ginger or jarred ginger root puree

¾ cup jarred garlic puree

½ cup ground cumin

2 tablespoons ground coriander

2 tablespoons crushed dried chiles (see Note)

4 cups lentils, preferably French green lentils

4 cups vegetable broth

4 cans (12 ounces each) chopped tomatoes with chiles

Lemon juice

Salt and freshly ground pepper

1. Melt the butter and sauté the onions, ginger, garlic, cumin, coriander, and chiles in a large pan over low to medium heat until the onions are translucent, about 10 minutes. Add the lentils and stir well to coat.

2. Stir in 3 quarts of water, the broth, and tomatoes. Increase the heat to high, bringing to a boil, then reduce the heat to low and put a lid on it. Cook for 1 hour, stirring gently every 15 minutes or so. See how the lentils are doing; they probably need another hour to get really soft.

3. Once the lentils are pretty soft, remove them from the heat and smoosh them with a fork or potato masher to break them up a bit. Add a little lemon juice and some salt and pepper to taste. You have to do it to taste, but lentils in my experience need a lot of salt.

Spicy Masala Chicken

First, to clarify, this is not chicken *marsala*. No, no it isn't.

This recipe originally called for marinating the chicken, but I was using frozen bone-in, skin-on chicken thighs that didn't require thawing before cooking. This option is cheap and just as flavorful as using boneless fresh thighs. The fat cooks out of them, and the skin comes off during cooking, so go for it if you are on a tight budget. Also, I didn't have the time or the space to marinate chicken for forty people, so I just basted the thighs with the marinade and it was really yummy. If you have time and space, go ahead and marinate the chicken for a few hours beforehand or even overnight. If you decide to marinate, don't reuse the marinade; reserve some ahead of time or make a new batch for the sauce. And don't substitute breast meat—it gets dry. You need a little extra fat for a good flavor.

FOR THE SAUCE/MARINADE

1 cup lemon juice

3 tablespoons jarred ginger puree

3 tablespoons jarred garlic puree

1 tablespoon crushed dried chiles

1 tablespoon salt

2 tablespoons molasses

4 tablespoons honey

FOR THE CHICKEN

20 pounds frozen chicken thighs, with bones and skin

TO MAKE THE SAUCE/MARINADE

In a small bowl, mix all of the ingredients together. Set aside.

TO MAKE THE CHICKEN

1. Preheat the grill to medium and your oven to 300°F.

2. Put the chicken thighs on the grill, still frozen, skin side up, over medium heat and close the lid. Grill for 10 minutes, watching for flare-ups as the fat drips down. (You don't want to burn down your

house while preparing for your dinner party; that's my definition of irony.)

3. After 10 minutes, transfer the chicken to a large baking pan (I needed three large pans, 9 by 12 inches, with high sides), and peel off the skin and excess fat using tongs. Spread the chicken out in a single layer with a slight overlap, to prevent the edges from getting overcooked and dried out during slow cooking.

4. Stab that chicken with a fork—go on, stab it all over. Then spread the sauce/marinade all over the chicken, using a basting brush or spoon so that you have enough for all of the pieces. Bake for 45 minutes, or until the thickest part of the thighs reaches 155°F. Remove and cover with foil. Let rest for 10 to 15 minutes. The chicken will continue to cook until done.

I am pretty laid back about hosting large gatherings, and I have a few things I do to make feeding a crowd faster and less stressful for everyone. Serving dinner buffet style is the only way to go. It is much easier to prepare platters in advance, set up quickly, and clean up at the end of the night. We certainly do not have tables and seating for forty in our tiny house, so guests sat on the floor, on cushions and blankets out in our yard, or stood around on the deck—which is why it was so important that everything was easy to eat with just a fork. I also made sure to have another area of the house designated for the bar, which left my kitchen counter clear to focus on the meal.

So that's it. The bulk of the food cost was the baby greens ($8), chicken ($25), and lentils ($5 or so); the rice was around $2; and everything was delicious! And honestly, it wasn't as stressful as I thought it was going to be. I had plenty of time to get showered and dressed before the guests started arriving, and more importantly, I had plenty of time to drink Champagne during the party. Cheers!

Glossary OF WEDDING TERMS AND ACRONYMS

Here's a little cheat-sheet to help you learn the slang so you can speak the language of weddings like it's your native tongue!

B-MAIDS: bridesmaids

BOUT: boutonniere, the dainty little floral doohickey the groom wears on his lapel

BROOCH BOUQUET: bridal bouquet composed of heirloom brooches rather than flowers

CHARGER: decorative platter that designates a place setting, which is either removed when plated food is served or remains underneath plated dishes as they are served

DIY: do it yourself

DOC: day-of coordinator, a wedding planner who mainly assists with day-of responsibilities; generally, this task also entails a few consultations pre-wedding

E-PARTY: engagement party

ESCORT CARD: printed card informing each guest at which table he or she will be seated

E-SESH: engagement photo session

FASCINATOR: accessory for the hair often worn to the side and composed of fabric, flowers, or feathers and embellishments, attached by a hair comb or hairclip

FH: future husband

FIRST LOOK: when the couple opts to see each other before the wedding ceremony and/or shoot group portraits during that time; often, the "first look" moment is documented by a photographer

FMIL: future mother-in-law; not to be confused with FML, which stands for something else entirely

FRIENDOR: wedding vendor who is also a friend—not necessarily a professional wedding vendor, but more frequently a friend who is talented in the ways of photography, planning and organizing, or general craftiness, and is willing to offer his or her services on your wedding day and beyond; friendors are generally compensated with love, traded services, or a little cash

HEN PARTY: bachelorette party (British terminology)

MIL: mother-in-law

MOB: mother of the bride

MOG: mother of the groom

MOH: maid or matron of honor

MUA: makeup artist

RECEIVING LINE: method of greeting each guest individually, in which the wedding party forms a line that the guests process through, usually directly following the ceremony

SECOND SHOOTER: additional photographer who provides alternate coverage for the lead photog

STAG PARTY: bachelor party (British terminology)

STDS: save-the-dates, in this case—notifications to your wedding guests that you are engaged to be married, on a specific day in a specific city, so they know to reserve the date on their calendar for your event; usually includes a wedding website URL or a line stating "formal invitation to follow"

TABLE NUMBER: signage that guests use to find their table, coordinating with the number or information on their escort card

VENDOR: professional offering services or goods related to wedding planning and execution

WEDDING OFFICIANT: person who, in almost every state, is legally required to marry you; the wedding officiant performs the ceremony and files your signed marriage license post-wedding, a mandatory step in officially getting married!

WEDDING PARTY: your bridesmaids and groomsmen, and flower girl(s) or ring bearer(s), if applicable (not to be confused with the rockin' party that will inevitably be following your ceremony—the reception)

WIC: Wedding Industrial Complex, aka The Media Machine, which you rage against every day, simply by being a Broke-Ass Bride

Resources

- **Style Me Pretty**
  www.stylemepretty.com
- **Green Wedding Shoes**
  www.greenweddingshoes.com
- **Wedding Chicks**
  www.weddingchicks.com
- **100 Layer Cake**
  www.100layercake.com/blog
- **Ruffled** www.ruffledblog.com
- **Snippet & Ink**
  www.snippetandink.com
- **Polka Dot Bride**
  www.polkadotbride.com
- **Emmaline Bride**
  emmalinebride.com
- **Once Wed** www.oncewed.com
- **Etsy Weddings**
  www.etsy.com/weddings
- **Oh Lovely Day**
  www.ohlovelyday.com
- **Every Last Detail**
  everylastdetailblog.com
- **Glamour & Grace**
  www.glamourandgraceblog.com
- **Ever Ours** www.ever-ours.com
- **The Knotty Bride**
  theknottybride.com
- **Heart Love Weddings**
  www.heartloveweddings.com
- **Junebug Weddings**
  junebugweddings.com
- **Brooklyn Bride**
  bklynbrideonline.com
- **The Storyboard Wedding**
  www.storyboardwedding.com
- **Grey Likes Weddings**
  www.greylikesweddings.com
- **Budget Fairy Tale**
  www.budgetfairytale.com
- **The Budget-Savvy Bride**
  thebudgetsavvybride.com
- **Elizabeth Anne Designs**
  elizabethannedesigns.com
- **Bride Ideas by Preston Bailey**
  brides.prestonbailey.com
- **Weddingbee**
  www.weddingbee.com
- **Offbeat Bride** offbeatbride.com
- **When Geeks Wed**
  whengeekswed.com
- **Rock n' Roll Bride**
  www.rocknrollbride.com
- **The Perfect Palette**
  www.theperfectpalette.com
- **Bitchless Bride**
  www.bitchlessbride.com
- **Eco-Beautiful Weddings**
  eco-beautifulweddings.com
- **Ritzy Bee** ritzybee.typepad.com
- **Mountainside Bride**
  mountainsidebride.com
- **Polka Dot Bride**
  www.polkadotbride.com
- **Valley & Co**
  www.valleyandcoblog.com
- **The Sweetest Occasion**
  www.thesweetestoccasion.com
- **Weddings Unveiled**
  www.weddingsunveiledmagazine
  .com
- **Staggered**
  www.iamstaggered.com
- **The Bride's Café**
  www.thebridescafe.com

- **Style Unveiled** styleunveiled.com
- **Merci New York**
  mercinewyork.com/blog
- **Always a Blogsmaid**
  alwaysablogsmaid.com
- **Rice Ink**
  www.momentaldesigns.com/
  rice-ink
- **Kiss My Tulle** www.kissmytulle.com
- **The Merriment Blog**
  www.merrimentevents.com/
  category/blog

BEST WEDDING BLOGS FOR WEDDING ADVICE, TIPS, AND SUPER-USEFUL ARTICLES

- **A Practical Wedding**
  apracticalwedding.com
- **Offbeat Bride** offbeatbride.com
- **HuffPost Weddings**
  www.huffingtonpost.com/weddings
- **Bitchless Bride**
  www.bitchlessbride.com
- **The Man Registry**
  www.themanregistry.com
- **The Budget Savvy Bride**
  thebudgetsavvybride.com
- **OneWed** www.onewed.com

BEST WEDDING MAGS (THAT ALSO HAVE TOTALLY AWESOME AND INFORMATIVE SITES OR BLOGS)

- **Brides/Brides.com**
  www.brides.com
- **Martha Stewart Weddings**
  www.MarthaStewartWeddings.com
- **The Knot** www.theknot.com
- **Eco-Beautiful Weddings**
  eco-beautifulweddings.com/blog
- **Southern Weddings**
  iloveswmag.com
- **Bridal Guide**
  www.bridalguide.com

BEST ORGANIZATIONAL SITES AND APPS

- **Pinterest** pinterest.com
- **Lover.ly** lover.ly
- **Luxefinds** luxefinds.com
- **Wedding Wire**
  www.weddingwire.com
- **WeddingVibe** weddingvibe.com
- **Appy Couple** appycouple.com
- **MyWedding.com**
  www.mywedding.com
- **Project Wedding**
  www.projectwedding.com

BEST CRAFTING SUPPLIES/ PRE-MADE SOURCES

- **Etsy** www.etsy.com
- **ArtFire** www.artfire.com
- **Michaels** www.michaels.com
  (always download the 20 percent off coupon before shopping!)
- **Oriental Trading Company**
  www.orientaltrading.com
- **SaveOnCrafts**
  www.save-on-crafts.com
- **Craigslist** craigslist.org
- **Freecycle** www.freecycle.org/

BEST WEDDING DRESS RESALE SITES

- **Tradesy**
  www.tradesy.com/weddings/
- **OwnedWeddingDresses.com**
  www.preownedweddingdresses
  .com/
- **EncoreBridal** encorebridal.com
- **OnceWed**
  www.oncewed.com/
  used-wedding-dresses/
- **BravoBride**
  www.bravobride.com
- **(and don't forget to check boards on your favorite wedding community sites!)**

Acknowledgments

Michael and Janet LaRue; Michael, Judith, and Grayson LaRue; Kim LaRue and Eric Holmgren; Dawn and Wayne Piper; Hunter Stiebel; Paco LaRue-Stiebel; Stacie Barra-Tournis; Andrew Paulson; Aliza Fogelson; Ashley Tucker; Emma Brodie; Sigi Nacson; Kevin Garcia; Zoe Chevat; Emily Anderson; Christen Moynihan; Melissa Leff; Liz Coopersmith; Paul Park; Brock Wilbur; Meg Keene; Tabitha Johnson; Rebecca Schenker; Brittany Hilgers; Mallory Murphy Viscardi; Robin Hitchcock; Lydia Yeung; Vanessa Oat Ghantous; Amber Marlow; Astrid Mueller; Lindsay Goldner; Michael Freeman; Max Piper; Candace and Matt Watters; Gerald, Penelope, and Danny Stiebel; Cathy Fiebach; Joey Honsa; Megan Hunt; Mindy Marzec; Anne Sage; Maggie Mason; Laura Mayes; Sarah Bryden-Brown; Lisa, Richard, and Veronica Ragsdale; Amber Gustafson; Jenny Lawson; Lewis Lain; Sarah Sassin Gray; Billy Gill and Karissa Vacker Gill; Ashley Rideaux; Sarah Bassak; Gail Baral; Sharon Naylor; Lara Casey; Millie Martini-Bratten; Stacie Ivers-Francombe; Sandie Ivers; Krissy Gasbarre; Robb Wain; Christel Winkler; Tom and Marlis Wilbur; Brooke Vinson; Mercedes Thurlbeck; Hank Olwell; Dorothea MacArthur; Drs. Brock Summers, Colin McCannel, Gary Holland, Simon Law, and Deborah Goldstein; Ann-Giselle Spiegler; Elizabeth Gilbert; Jonathan Safran Foer; Rick Bayless; Coca-Cola Corporation; Kraft Macaroni and Cheese; 7-11; the creative staff and actors behind *Law & Order(s): SVU* and *Criminal Intent*; and the entire staff at Random House/Potter Style.

Each of you has helped shape me into the artist I am. Thank you from the bottom of my heart. For loving me. For supporting me. For inspiring me. For keeping me safe. For preserving my health. For keeping me sane. For feeding me. For teaching me. For guiding me. For loving me. For being yourselves. Your fabulous, one-of-a-kind selves. Thank you from the very bottom of my heart.

Index